THE WRATH OF
SPARKY

Also by Tom Tomorrow

Greetings from This Modern World
Tune in Tomorrow

THE WRATH OF SPARKY

ST. MARTIN'S GRIFFIN ≈ NEW YORK

Design and production by Dan Perkins
Cover design by Dan Perkins and Dave Eggers
Back cover photograph by Tom Erikson/stained glass Sparky by Phyllis Hulvey

Write Tom Tomorrow c/o Keith Kahla
St. Martin's Press
175 Fifth Avenue
New York, N.Y. 10010

or e-mail: tomorrow@well.com

and if you're on the net, visit the Tom Tomorrow web site:
http://www.well.com/user/tomorrow

Several Tom Tomorrow t-shirt designs (including Sparky for President) are available from:

Post Industrial Stress Design
2506 S. Fawcett
Tacoma, WA 98402
800-331-7173
email: PISD@aol.com

Library of Congress Cataloging-in-Publication Data

Tomorrow, Tom
The wrath of Sparky by Tom Tomorrow.
p.   cm.
ISBN 0-312-13753-2
1. United States—Politics and government—1993—Caricatures and
cartoons.   2. American wit and humor, Pictorial.   I. Title.
E885.T65   1996
741.5'973—dc20   96-7286   CIP

First St. Martin's Griffin Edition: August 1996

10   9   8   7   6   5   4   3   2   1

ACKNOWLEDGMENTS

In addition to the thousand or so people I'm going to remember as soon as this book hits the press, I want to thank: Tony Auth, Ben Bagdikian, Jello Biafra, Nicholas Blechman, Kimberly Burns, Noam Chomsky, Norman Davis, Bruce Dobie, Susan Ellis, Tom Erickson, Jules Feiffer, Michael Finger, Dennis Freeland, Gerry Fren, Kathi Goldmark, Jim Gorman, Barry Greenhut, Bill Griffith, Steve Hamilton, Ray Hartmann, Greg Horne, Carl Jensen, Jocelyn Joson, Jonathan Lethem, Mark Lowenthal, Paul Mavrides (for fighting the good fight, and winning), Steve Moss, A. Lin Neumann, Franny Nudelman, Jeff O'Connell, Nanci O'Dea, Joel Pett, Bruce Schimmel, Amy Shuck, Larry Smith, Winston Smith, J. R. Swanson, Christine Triano, Katrina Vanden Heuvel, Melinda Welsh, Ty Wenger, and Thom Zajac. They all helped out in one way or another, though some of them may not have realized how much it mattered.

Particular thanks are due to Signe Wilkenson, for her help and advocacy, not to mention her efforts as my unofficial travel agent over the past year; to Dave Eggers, without whose above-and-beyond efforts this book would probably not have a cover; to Steve Rhodes, webmaster extraordinaire (whose handiwork can be seen at www.well.com/user/tomorrow); and finally to Keith Kahla, who is largely responsible for the somewhat unlikely fact that these books of mine continue to be published.

This one is dedicated to Beverly, for grace bestowed.

FOREWORD

Inspired by the first few months of the 104th Congress, I was originally thinking about calling this book *Republicans Are Scum Sucking Vermin (More Gentle Wit and Good Natured Humor from America's Most Heartwarming Cartoonist)*. Contrary to what you might expect, my publishers loved the idea—I actually had to talk *them* out of it after I had second (and third and fourth) thoughts. One problem was that Al Franken had just released *Rush Limbaugh Is a Big Fat Idiot,* which was essentially the same joke, and he got it into print first. But more importantly, I began to think about how much mail I already get from clue-impaired readers who seem to believe that I am little more than an obedient foot soldier marching in lockstep with the Democratic National Committee (alongside all my comrades in the monolithic liberal media, of course). One such correspondent, for instance, recently advised me via e-mail to "stand up for normal American values like marriage, heterosexuality, Christianity, and the old-fashioned work ethic and stop writing like a disgruntled child or welfare mama. You may be unhappy about it, but most of America is normal and conservative, unlike East and West Coast weirdos and the draft-dodging 'President.'" Another e-mail pal (and gosh, I sure have my share of them) wrote: "You are nothing but a partisan flack for the Taxicratic Party. The best thing about your cartoon is that it does get people thinking. This is where you made your big mistake. Because facts refute Liberalism every time. While you may think you are getting people all charged up to vote Democrat, sooner or later, if they continue to search for the truth, they will eventually come around." You can just imagine my dismay at the exposure of my secret plan to rally the cartoon-reading public around the centrist, pro-business Clinton agenda.

Yes, I target Republicans more frequently than Democrats—how can any honest satirist not focus on a party that so shamelessly champions polluted air, dirty water, and poisoned meat on behalf of their corporate benefactors?—but this does *not* mean I am blindly in favor of any idiotic corporate sellout the *Democrats* propose. Despite what the diddleheads want to believe, life isn't that simple. In the foreword to my last book, I discussed my own sense that the real conflict in this country "has nothing to do with right or left, conservative or liberal; it has everything to do with up or down, ruling or working class." In the two years since I wrote those words it has become somewhat more acceptable to discuss the ongoing class war being fought (and won) by the rich and privileged against the rest of the population, but it's taken Pat Buchanan, of all people, to bring the issue to the table. And meanwhile, having been forced to admit that a problem might even exist, TV pundits and other defenders of the status quo are working overtime to convince Americans that the problem isn't with the nature of modern-day capitalism, isn't with a politically autonomous Fed chairman who seems determined to choke off any hint of job growth in his Don Quixote-ish battle against inflationary threats only he can perceive, and certainly isn't with corporations which act as if they have no obligation whatsoever to the society in which they are allowed to exist—the problem is, in fact, with American workers themselves! If you lose your job because your company downsizes to appease Wall Street, the pundits helpfully explain, it's your own damned fault! You just don't have the skills required to compete in the fabulous new information economy! Oddly enough, as large companies continue to reduce their workforces while simultaneously posting record profits, Americans seem dubious that a little retraining and a subscription to *Wired* magazine are all they need to keep their heads above water. AT&T received so much bad publicity for its recently announced layoffs that it was forced to place full-page ads in *The New York Times* and *USA Today* imploring other companies to hire their former employees—which, come to think of it, pretty much sums up the *fin-de-siècle* corporate credo: "Will somebody *else* please give these people jobs so they can afford to pay for *our* goods and services?" You don't have to have an advanced degree in economics to see that there's something wrong with that—in fact, given the pronouncements of most economists, it's probably better if you don't. The question, of course, is what can possibly be done—and frankly, I don't have the slightest idea. But (if you'll excuse the cliché) I do know this: You can't have a debate about what the emperor should wear until somebody points out that the emperor is naked, and that's what I figure I'm being paid to do. So listen up, folks: Clinton, Dole, Gingrich, Limbaugh, Greenspan, most of the 104th Congress, and just about every so-called expert yammering away on TV every night . . . they're all naked, every goddammed one of them, right down to their flabby white buttocks.

And I'll tell you, it's not a pretty sight.

About this book: Most of the following cartoons are, of course, taken from my weekly self-syndicated feature, *This Modern World,* which appears regularly in about 100 newspapers—a fact that astonishes me as much as anyone, particularly given *TMW*'s extremely humble beginnings as a self-published 'zine a decade ago, when I began to experiment with combining my interests in cartooning and collage. The result was a story satirizing consumerism and technology, which was later reprinted in *Processed World* and (in a slightly altered form) a comic book called *Centrifugal Bubble Puppy.* I went to the trouble of digging the latter version out of the voluminous and dust-filled Tom Tomorrow archives because no effort is too great for you, the reader (and because we had some space to kill in this book). It's reprinted on pages 32–45, and while I had to resist the urge to clean it up here and there, I think it still holds up relatively well and hope it may be of some interest to readers curious about the evolution of my work. One thing that strikes me in retrospect is the degree to which random chance dictated the story, many parts of which were written solely because I happened to have come across a strange image I wanted to include. (The peculiar meeting between Bill and his boss, for instance, was inspired by an old Timex ad picturing the watch-wearing turtles I incorporated into the background.) I should also note that I cannibalized this story somewhat when I began to work on turning *This Modern World* into a weekly newspaper cartoon; readers with long memories may remember some of these panels as single cartoons from my first book, *Greetings from This Modern World.*

There are a few other oddities and rarities in this book as well. "The Trouble with Brains" (page 52) originally appeared in color on the Endpaper page of *The New York Times Sunday Magazine.* (And if it had occurred to me to think about it at all when I was working on that aforementioned 'zine, I would have figured I had about as much chance of getting into *The New York Times* as, well, turtles have of knowing the correct time.)

The Sparkymobile on pages 60–63 was something I designed for fun a few years ago and has never appeared in print anywhere. (A note about that: Certain national copy center franchises have been cowed by lawsuits and will refuse to make even single copies of copyrighted material without specific permission from the copyright holder, so if you're one of the three readers who is actually going to try to build the model, just show them this paragraph in which I SPECIFICALLY GIVE THE HOLDER OF THIS BOOK PERMISSION TO COPY PAGES 60–63—OKAY, KINKO'S?) (Not that explaining the concept of a pen name every time I want to make a copy of my own damn work has left me irritable or annoyed, you understand.)

The somewhat squashed-looking cartoons on pages 100–101 and 112–113 originally appeared on the letters page of *The Nation,* to which I have been contributing an original cartoon once a month since their recent redesign, much to the dismay of many longtime subscribers who can't believe what the world is coming to. (Numerous ads for spanking erotica can still be found on the magazine's classified page, so at least some traditions remain unsullied.)

Finally, the stained glass Sparky I'm holding on the back cover photograph was made for me as a birthday present in 1993 by my mom, who was killed by a drunk driver later the same year.

—Dan Perkins
("Tom Tomorrow")
San Francisco
April, 1996

INTRODUCTION by A. Friend
(an actual letter from an actual reader)

May 13, 1994

Dummkopf Tom Tomorrow
Des Moines Register
Des Moines, Iowa

Dear Dummkopf and general all-around Nuisance,

    Recently I saw your asinine cartoon against our beloved President Nixon. Your cartoon was very biased and stupid. Try not to show your stupidity in the future. Fall on your knees and ask the good Lord to give you a little common sense, Brother, you need it. People feel sorry for you.

    Some say you are a Mongolian idiot! I have been defending you against the charge. Oh, ho, ho, ho! Oh, ha, ha, ha!

    Have you no sense of shame and decency? Those who know you and work with you complain about your personal habits. They need a gas mask when they are around you. Take a bath daily and try to avoid gaseous foods in the future.

    Good bye for now, Dummkopf.

Sincerely,
A. Friend
A. Friend

Editor's note: the cartoon to which Mr. (or Ms.) Friend refers appears on page 2 of this book.

THIS MODERN WORLD by TOM TOMORROW

AMERICANS **WORSHIP** POLLS AND STATIS- TICS...NEVER DOUBTING FOR A MOMENT THAT A FEW THOUSAND INTERVIEWS CAN BE USED TO ACCURATELY EXTRAPOLATE THE INNERMOST SECRETS OF A NATION OF 253 **MILLION** PEOPLE...

HEY HONEY--WANT SOME **COTTAGE CHEESE**? 56% OF AMERICANS CAN'T LIVE WITH- OUT IT!

NO THANKS! LIKE 83.5% OF OUR FELLOW CITIZENS, I DON'T HAVE **TIME** FOR BREAKFAST!

...SO IT IS NO SURPRISE THAT THE RESULTS OF THE NEW **SEX SURVEY** HAVE BEEN SO QUICKLY EMBRACED BY RATIONAL THINK- ERS EVERYWHERE...

...INCLUDING THE EDITORS OF CER- TAIN **NEWSMAGAZINES**...

...WHO SEEMED SUSPICIOUSLY **PLEASED** TO REPORT THAT **BORING SEX** IS THE **NORM**...

TIME

ACCORDING TO THE STUDY, ONLY 54% OF AMERICAN MEN-- AND **19%** OF WOMEN-- EVEN GIVE A PASSING **THOUGHT** TO SEX ON ANY GIVEN DAY...

SEX? SWEATY, PANTING, SHUD- DERING **SEX?!**

NOPE, CAN'T SAY I THINK ABOUT **THAT** MUCH!

I'M MUCH TOO BUSY KNITTING **MACRAME ANI- MALS** TO THINK ABOUT THAT SORT OF THING!

FACT OR FICTION, THESE NUMBERS WILL BE BANDIED ABOUT ON NEWS PROGRAMS AND TALK SHOWS FOR **YEARS**-- OR AT LEAST UNTIL THE **NEXT** POLL IS RE- LEASED...

WHY--IT SAYS HERE THAT 94% OF AMER- ICANS HAVE HAD SEX WITH THEIR **KITCHEN APPLIANCES!**

WELL, IF IT SAYS SO IN A SURVEY THEN IT **MUST** BE TRUE!

TOM·RROW @11·9·94

1

THIS MODERN WORLD
by TOM TOMORROW

Panel 1:

LAST WEEK, RICHARD NIXON--A MAN WHO NEEDLESSLY PROLONGED AN EVIL WAR FOR YEARS--WAS LAID TO REST BENEATH A TOMBSTONE DECLARING HIM A *"PEACEMAKER"*...

--AND WITH PEACEMAKERS LIKE *THIS*, WHO NEEDS *WARMONGERS?*

Panel 2:

POSTHUMOUS MEDIA COMMENTARY CONSISTED PRIMARILY OF FLUFFY EULOGIES WHICH GLOSSED OVER VIETNAM AND WATERGATE IN FAVOR OF *PLEASANT GENERALITIES*...

HE WAS--UM--*CONTROVERSIAL*... BUT ONE THING'S FOR SURE-- HE WAS BORN IN *YORBA LINDA!*

YES--AND FEW WOULD DENY THAT HE WAS OUR *THIRTY-SEVENTH* PRESIDENT!

ACTION McNEWS

Panel 3:

IT WAS, UNDOUBTEDLY, THE RESULT OF A WELL-INTENTIONED DESIRE TO SPEAK NO ILL OF THE DEAD...AFTER ALL, RICHARD NIXON'S SINS ARE HISTORY *NOW*, RIGHT?

LET BYGONES BE BYGONES, THAT'S WHAT *I* SAY!

YEAH! WHAT'S TH' BIG DEAL ABOUT A CONSTITUTIONAL CRISIS AND A MULTITUDE OF WAR DEAD ANYWAY?

Panel 4:

OF COURSE, WHY STOP WITH *NIXON?* HECK, IF YOU CAN'T SAY SOMETHING *NICE* ABOUT A DEAD PERSON--*ANY* DEAD PERSON--THEN DON'T SAY ANYTHING AT *ALL!*

AL CAPONE WAS QUITE A *MARKSMAN!*

THE AYATOLLAH KHOMEINI WAS *VERY SPIRITUAL!*

THAT LIZZIE BORDEN SURE KNEW HOW TO EXPRESS HER *FEELINGS!*

TOM TOMORROW © 5-11-94

2

THIS MODERN WORLD by TOM TOMORROW

DOES A CIVILIZED SOCIETY HAVE A MORAL OB-LIGATION TO ENSURE ACCESS TO HEALTH CARE FOR EVERYONE? MANY PEOPLE SEEM NOT TO THINK SO...

HEY--HEALTH CARE IS JUST *ANOTHER CONSUMER COMMODITY!* YOU DON'T SEE THE GOVERNMENT GOING AROUND HANDING OUT *FREE CADILLACS,* DO YOU?

GOSH-- I SURE CAN'T ARGUE WITH LOGIC LIKE *THAT!*

OF COURSE, MANY PEOPLE HAVE FORMED STRONG OPINIONS ON THE BASIS OF *IN-SURANCE INDUSTRY COMMERCIALS* AND *RUSH LIMBAUGH DIATRIBES*...AND LIT-TLE *ELSE*...

--AND IF YOU TRY TO SEE A DOCTOR WITHOUT A *BUREAUCRAT'S PER-MISSION,* YOU'LL BE THROWN IN *JAIL!*

THAT'S *AWFUL!*

ONE LIMBAUGH LISTENER, APPARENTLY UN-AWARE OF THE INHERENT FRAGILITY OF HU-MAN EXISTENCE, ACTUALLY HAD *THIS* TO SAY ON THE SUBJECT:

RUSH, WE DON'T NEED HEALTH CARE REFORM--

THERE *JUST AREN'T THAT MANY SICK PEOPLE!*

THE MISINFORMED AND IGNORANT WILL NOT *DECIDE* THIS DEBATE, BUT THEY *WILL* INFLUENCE IT...AND CHANCES ARE THAT ANY REFORM BILL WHICH ACTUALLY *PASSES* WILL BE SOMEWHAT LESS *COM-PREHENSIVE* THAN INITIALLY PROMISED...

UNDER THIS *HISTORIC LEGISLATION,* EVERY AMERICAN WILL RECEIVE ONE OF THESE HEALTH SECURITY *COUPONS*--

--GOOD FOR *50¢ OFF* A BOTTLE OF *ASPIRIN* OR A PACKAGE OF *BAND-AIDS!*

HEALTH SECURITY 250¢

TOM TOMORROW©8-3-94

3

THIS MODERN WORLD by TOM TOMORROW

PERHAPS AMERICA COULD *LEARN* A THING OR TWO FROM SINGAPORE.

I *AGREE*, BIFF! I THINK A FEW *CANINGS* MIGHT RESTORE A LITTLE RESPECT FOR THE *LAW* IN THIS COUNTRY!

YOU DO?

SURE! WHY I'LL BET THE CEO OF *GENERAL ELECTRIC* WOULD THINK TWICE ABOUT *DEFRAUDING THE GOVERNMENT* IF THE PENALTY WERE A GOOD, SOUND *FLOGGING*!

AND MAYBE IF HE'D BEEN WORRIED ABOUT PROTECTING HIS TUSH IN A MORE *LITERAL SENSE*, *OLIVER NORTH* WOULDN'T HAVE BEEN SO QUICK TO SET UP A *GUN RUNNING* OPERATION IN THE WHITE HOUSE *BASEMENT*!

FOR THAT MATTER, A BARE-BOTTOM SPANKING MIGHT BE JUST THE THING FOR *RUSH LIMBAUGH*! I THINK IT'S *DREADFUL* HOW HE FLOUTS HIS DISRESPECT FOR THE LAW--AND OPENLY ADMITS SMOKING *ILLEGAL CUBAN CIGARS*!

AFTER ALL, THE *LAW* IS THE *LAW*... RIGHT, BIFF?

≋SIGH≋...I DON'T KNOW WHY I BOTHER TALKING TO YOU.

4

THIS MODERN WORLD
by TOM TOMORROW

IT'S *WIRED* --THE MAGAZINE ABOUT NEW FORMS OF COMMUNICATION WHOSE WACKY USE OF TYPE AND BACKGROUNDS OFTEN RENDERS IT *COMPLETELY UNREADABLE*...

OH, DON'T BE SUCH A *LUDDITE!*

YES-- *CONTENT* IS SO *OLD-FASHIONED!* WHAT MATTERS IN THE *INFORMATION AGE* ...IS *LAYOUT!*

WIRED CELEBRATES ITS SUBJECT WITH *GUSTO!* AS ONE EDITOR RECENTLY COMMENTED, "TECHNOLOGY IS NOT NEUTRAL--TECHNOLOGY IS ABSOLUTELY 100% POSITIVE!"

HMM-- SO THE DISTRESS I AM CURRENTLY EXPERIENCING--

--IS SIMPLY THE RESULT OF YOUR OUTMODED "SECOND WAVE" THINKING!

WIRED IS TO THE NINETIES WHAT *PLAYBOY* WAS TO THE SIXTIES--A MAGAZINE LARGELY DEVOTED TO CONVINCING IMPRESSIONABLE YOUNG MEN THAT *NOTHING* IS HIPPER THAN BEING A *GOOD CONSUMER*...

IF I ONLY HAD A QUADROPHONIC HI-FI SYSTEM-- *THEN* I'D GET THE BABES!

IF I ONLY HAD A POWERFUL MULTIMEDIA SYSTEM-- *THEN* I'D GET THE BABES!

OF COURSE, *WIRED* IS ULTIMATELY MORE THAN A MERE *MAGAZINE*--IT'S A *WAY OF LIFE*...NOT UNLIKE, SAY, THE *UNIFICATION CHURCH*...

YOU SIMPLY DON'T UNDERSTAND OUR ADVANCED PARADIGM.

WE SCORN AND PITY YOU.

WOULD YOU LIKE TO BUY A COPY OF OUR *NEW ISSUE*?

TOM TOMORROW © 11-22-95

THIS MODERN WORLD

by TOM TOMORROW

OKAY... WE UNDERSTAND WHY SO MANY TV VIEWERS WERE TRANSFIXED BY THE L.A.P.D.'S PURSUIT OF O.J. SIMPSON... IT WAS, AFTER ALL, A BIZARRE, UNFOLDING DRAMA WITH A HIGHLY UNCERTAIN OUTCOME...

--AND ANYWAY, WHAT COULD *POSSIBLY* BE MORE COMPELLING THAN WATCHING A WHITE BRONCO DRIVE DOWN THE FREEWAY FOR *FOUR HOURS*?

WHAT'S YOUR *POINT*?

OJ DAILY NEWS
OJ SNEEZES

...BUT WAS IT *REALLY* NECESSARY FOR EVERY MEDIA ORGANIZATION IN THE *COUNTRY* TO PROVIDE BLOW-BY-BLOW COVERAGE OF THE SUBSEQUENT PRE-TRIAL HEARING..?

THIS IS BIFF WILLIAMS AT THE L.A. COUNTY COURTHOUSE-- WHERE THE JUDGE JUST TOOK A *BATHROOM BREAK*!

BIFF--HOW LONG WAS SHE *IN* THE BATHROOM?

OF COURSE, THE MEDIA THEMSELVES HAVE BEEN ASKING THIS QUESTION-- AS A WAY TO JUSTIFY SPENDING EVEN *MORE* TIME ON THE STORY, THAT IS...

COMING UP NEXT-- A SPECIAL *SEVEN HOUR LOOK* AT THE *COVERAGE* OF THE *COVERAGE* OF THE *O.J. SIMPSON CASE!* -- BUT FIRST, A BRIEF REPORT ON THE DEATH OF KIM IL-SUNG.

WHAT-- DID *HE* KNOW O.J.?

IT'S PROBABLY JUST GOING TO GET *WORSE*... WHY, JUST CONSIDER WHAT MIGHT HAVE HAPPENED IF THE MERGER OF CBS AND QVC HAD ACTUALLY GONE THROUGH...

--AND CONNIE, THIS *GENUINE COPY* OF O.J.'S MUG SHOT IS MOUNTED ON A *REAL WOOD PLAQUE*!

SOURCES SAY IT'S A *REAL VALUE* AT ONLY $49.95, DAN!

6

THIS MODERN WORLD
by TOM TOMORROW

HYPOCRISY KNOWS NO IDEOLOGICAL BOUNDS... AS HAS BEEN MADE CLEAR BY THE NUMEROUS APOLOGISTS FOR INDICTED FORMER WAYS AND MEANS CHAIR *DAN ROSTENKOWSKI*...

YOU SEE, HE IS FROM A *DIFFERENT ERA!*

AND ANYWAY, THAT'S JUST HOW THEY DO THINGS IN CHICAGO!

WELL-- THAT EX- PLAINS *EVERY- THING!*

...AS WELL AS ALMOST *EVERYONE'S* RESPONSE TO PAULA JONES...FROM CONSERVATIVES WHO HAVE SUDDENLY BECOME *ARDENT FEMI- NISTS*...TO LIBERALS WHO SUDDENLY SOUND LIKE *DITTOHEADS*...

THIS--THIS IS AN *OUTRAGE!* THIS POOR WOMAN HAS BEEN *SEXUALLY HARASSED!* SHE HAS BEEN *DISEMPOW- ERED!*

AAAH-- SHE WAS ASKING FOR IT!

IN OTHER RECENT POLITICAL WACKINESS, VIR- GINIA REPUBLICANS HAVE OFFICIALLY CHO- SEN *OLIVER NORTH* AS THEIR CANDIDATE FOR SENATE...

--AND WHAT CAN WE REALLY *ADD* TO THAT?

REALITY HAS SURPASSED *SATIRE* HERE, FOLKS...

FINALLY, WE'D LIKE TO NOTE THE OPENING OF A CERTAIN SUMMER MOVIE...WHICH WILL UNDOUBTEDLY PROVIDE AN EASY THEME FOR EVERY EDITORIAL CARTOONIST IN THE *COUNTRY* IN THE WEEKS TO COME...

♪CLINTSTONES... MEET THE *CLINTSTONES*♪

HIL-MA! I'M *HO-OME!*

YABBA DABBA DOO!

...NOT THAT *WE* WOULD EVER STOOP SO LOW...

TOM TOMORROW © 6-15-94

THIS MODERN WORLD
by TOM TOMORROW

Panel 1:
YOU'RE ENTERING A STRANGE DIMENSION... WHERE *SUBSTANCE* IS IRRELEVANT... AND *IMAGE* REIGNS SUPREME...

$E = mc^2$

Panel 2:
...A DIMENSION WHERE REPORTERS ARE PAID EXHORBITANT SALARIES TO BARK *SUPERFICIAL QUESTIONS* AT ADMINISTRATION *FLACKS*...

DEE DEE--

DEE DEE--

DEE DEE--WHAT IS THE PRESIDENT'S POLICY ON--ER--THE *ISSUES?*

PRESS

Panel 3:
...AND WHERE JOURNALISM IS LARGELY LIMITED TO VERBATIM REPORTS OF *EVASIVE OFFICIAL DOUBLESPEAK*...

WELL, THE PRESIDENT IS VERY *CONCERNED* ABOUT THE ISSUES...AND INTENDS TO BEGIN TO THINK ABOUT ADDRESSING THEM SOMETIME IN THE INDETERMINATE FUTURE!--NEXT QUESTION?

DEE DEE--

DEE DEE--

DEE DEE--

Tom Tomorrow © 8-7-94

Panel 4:
YES...YOU'RE ENTERING THE...

WASHINGTON PRESS ZONE...

GOD HELP YOU...

DEE DEE--

DEE DEE--

DEE DEE DEE DEE DEE DEE DEE DEE DEE DEE DEE

THIS MODERN WORLD
by TOM TOMORROW

THOUGH THE NEED FOR CAMPAIGN REFORM IS OFTEN GIVEN LIP SERVICE, MOST POLITICIANS NOT ONLY *ACCEPT* SPECIAL INTEREST MONEY-- THEY ACTIVELY *SOLICIT* IT...

FATTON, HOGGS & DOUGH

SENATOR! HOW NICE TO *HEAR* FROM YOU!

AH--*CERTAINLY!* RIGHT AWAY!

SMALL *UNMARKED* BILLS, YOU SAY?

AND YET...THEY MUST STILL TRY TO PORTRAY THEM-SELVES AS *SELFLESS PUBLIC SERVANTS*...HIDING THEIR SUBSERVIENCE TO THEIR CAMPAIGN CON-TRIBUTORS BEHIND A SMOKESCREEN OF *MEAN-INGLESS BUZZWORDS*...

SENATOR--DO YOU *REALLY* THINK IT'S A GOOD IDEA TO ELIMINATE *ALL* CORPORATE TAXES?

ABSOLUTELY! YOU SEE-- THE *FREE MARKET! JOB CREATION! BLATHER! BLA-THER! BLATHER!*

...AS WELL AS OFFERING UP *SCAPEGOATS* TO DISTRACT ATTENTION...PREFERABLY ONES THAT ARE *WEAK* AND *POWERLESS*...

ANYWAY, WHY MUST WE FOCUS SO OB-SESSIVELY ON *CORPORATE AMERICA*? WHY, WE COULD WIPE OUT THE DEFICIT *TOMORROW*--IF *CHILDREN* PAID TAX-ES ON THEIR *ALLOWANCES!*

THESE LITTLE FREELOADERS ARE COSTING US *BILLIONS!*

WITH A LITTLE HELP FROM A COMPLIANT MEDIA, THE PUBLIC'S ATTENTION IS SUITABLY MISDIRECTED...ALLOWING THE *REAL* BUSINESS OF RUNNING THE COUNTRY TO CONTINUE *UNFETTERED*...

GRR.

SO YOU ALSO WANT TO LOWER THE MINIMUM WAGE TO *TWELVE CENTS* AN *HOUR?*

THAT'S RIGHT! YOU SEE-- *COMPETITIVE-NESS!* THE *GLOBAL ECONOMY!*

Daily Record

KIDS DODGE TAXES!

DEFICIT THEIR FAULT

?

THIS MODERN WORLD by TOM TOMORROW

Panel 1: REPUBLICANS ACT AS IF THE IDEA OF UNIVERSAL ACCESS TO HEALTH CARE IS SOMEHOW *SINISTER* AND *UNAMERICAN*...

COMMUNISM MAY BE DEAD *HERE*, COMRADE-- BUT SOON...SOON...AMERICANS WILL BE ABLE TO GET MEDICAL TREATMENT WHEN THEY ARE SICK--EVEN IF THEY ARE *POOR* OR *UNEMPLOYED*!

HEH! AND THEY THINK *THEY* WON THE COLD WAR!

THE *FOOLS*!

Panel 2: THEY RESPOND TO EACH DEMOCRATIC PROPOSAL--NO MATTER HOW WATERED-DOWN--WITH THE SAME TIRESOME REFRAIN OF "SOCIALIZED MEDICINE"...

..THOUGH I HAVEN'T HEARD ANYONE COMPLAINING LATELY ABOUT "SOCIALIZED *ROADS*"...OR "SOCIALIZED *POLICE DEPARTMENTS*"...

I GUESS "SOCIALISM" IS IN THE EYE OF THE *BEHOLDER*...

Panel 3: CONSERVATIVE COMMENTATORS ARE WORKING HARD TO CONVINCE AMERICANS THAT HEALTH CARE IS NOT A *NECESSITY*, BUT RATHER-- IN THE WORDS OF OUR FRIEND RUSH LIMBAUGH--"AN *OPTION*"...

HEY RUSH! *I* DON'T NEED ANY HEALTH CARE REFORM! I'M GONNA STUDY MEDICINE IN MY SPARE TIME--AND IF I GET *SICK*, I'LL JUST OPERATE ON *MYSELF*!

THAT'S THE SPIRIT!

SEE I TOLD YOU SO
HOOKED ON PHONICS

Panel 4: OF COURSE, THE G.O.P. CAN'T AFFORD TO APPEAR *COMPLETELY* OBSTRUCTIONIST... SO THEY *HAVE* OFFERED SOME HELPFUL IDEAS OF THEIR OWN...

--AND WE WOULDN'T NEED ANY REFORM AT *ALL*-- IF THE UNINSURED WOULD JUST BECOME *CHRISTIAN SCIENTISTS*!

THEY DON'T GO TO DOCTORS, YOU KNOW!

HERE--HAVE A BROCHURE!

TOM TOMORROW © 8-31-94

10

THIS MODERN WORLD

by TOM TOMORROW

STEP ONE: HIRE A FOLKSY, HOMESPUN NARRATOR.

WELL, AH DON'T KNOW TOO MUCH 'BOUT WHAT GOES ON UP THERE IN WARSHINGTON D.C....

STEP TWO: HAVE HIM DESCRIBE SOME PENDING BIT OF LEGISLATION IN TERMS THAT ARE AS VAGUE AS THEY ARE ALARMING.

...BUT AH DO KNOW THAT IF THEY PASS THAT NEW LAW 'BOUT THE TAXES AN' STUFF-- WELL, IT'S GONNA MEAN THE END OF LIFE AS WE KNOW IT!

AH GUESS CONGRESS JUST DON'T CARE 'BOUT ENDIN' LIFE AS WE KNOW IT!

STEP THREE: PROVIDE A TOLL-FREE NUMBER CITIZENS CAN CALL TO EXPRESS THEIR NEW-FOUND CONCERN.

DON'T LET CONGRESS END LIFE AS WE KNOW IT!

1-800-STOP-EM

PAID FOR BY THE COALITION TO PRESERVE LIFE AS WE KNOW IT!

STEP FOUR: VOILA! IT'S DEMOCRACY IN THE NINETIES!

WHY--THAT'S SIMPLY AWFUL--WHATEVER IT IS CONGRESS WANTS TO DO!

YES! WE'D BETTER CALL RIGHT AWAY!

TOM TOMORROW © 8-30-95

11

THIS MODERN WORLD by TOM TOMORROW

MR. GORE-- *REPORT!*

THE BEINGS APPEAR TO HAVE SUBMERGED THEIR INDIVIDUAL IDENTITIES INTO A COLLECTIVE *HIVE CONSCIOUSNESS,* CAPTAIN...

THEY SEEM TO INHABIT A SELF-CONTAINED BUBBLE OF *ALTERNATE REALITY,* COMPLETELY UNAFFECTED BY THE LAWS OF *OUR* UNIVERSE... LOGIC AND RATIONALITY ARE *IRRELEVANT* TO THEM...

THEY ARE LINKED TO ONE ANOTHER BY AUDIO TRANSMISSIONS WHICH RELAY THE INCESSANT BABBLING OF AN OTHERWISE UNEXCEPTIONAL MEMBER OF THEIR SPECIES--WHO IS, IN RETURN, FED AND PAMPERED LIKE THE BLOATED QUEEN OF A *TERMITE COLONY...*

MY *GOD*-- YOU MEAN--?

YES, CAP-TAIN--

--THEY ARE *DITTOHEADS...*

YOU WILL BE *ASSIMILATED.*

RESISTANCE IS *FUTILE.*

DITTOS.

DITTOS.

DITTOS.

DITTOS.

MEGA-DITTOS.

12

THIS MODERN WORLD
by TOM TOMORROW

POLITICIANS ARE PROFESSING **OUTRAGE** AT THE DISCOVERY OF A RUSSIAN SPY IN THE CIA... EVEN THOUGH INTELLIGENCE SOURCES CONCEDE THAT THE CIA CONTINUES TO SPY ON **RUSSIA**...

WELL THAT'S **DIFFERENT**-- BECAUSE-- UM-- BECAUSE--

--BECAUSE WE'RE **AMERICANS!**

RICK AMES IS ACCUSED OF BETRAYING HIS COUNTRY FOR FINANCIAL GAIN -- BY REVEALING THE NAMES OF SOVIET CITIZENS WHO WERE WORKING FOR THE CIA...

--SOVIETS WHO WERE, IN OTHER WORDS, BETRAYING **THEIR** COUNTRY--PRESUMABLY FOR FINANCIAL GAIN...

FRANKLY I'M NOT SURE **ANYONE** SHOULD BE LAYING CLAIM TO THE MORAL **HIGH GROUND** HERE...

IT TOOK THE CIA ALMOST TEN YEARS TO GROW SUSPICIOUS OF AMES...WHO MADE $70,000 A YEAR, AND YET LIVED IN A $540,000 **HOME**, DROVE A $65,000 **JAGUAR**, AND FREQUENTLY TRAVELLED **OVERSEAS**...

HEY-- I JUST KNOW HOW TO **BUDGET!**

TO DO
PICK UP LAUNDRY
DEPOSIT KGB PAYOFF
RETURN VIDEO

$ $ $

OF COURSE, THIS **IS** THE SAME INTELLIGENCE AGENCY WHICH WAS CAUGHT UNAWARES BY THE COLLAPSE OF THE SOVIET UNION...AND GOD ONLY KNOWS WHAT **ELSE**...

SIR, I'VE BEEN ANALYZING THE DATA-- AND APPARENTLY GEORGE BUSH LOST THE '92 ELECTION! A MAN NAMED **BILL CLINTON** IS NOW PRESIDENT!

CLINTON, EH? I'LL NOTIFY THE DIRECTOR **IMMEDIATELY!**

MARCH 1994

TOP SECRET

TOM TOMORROW ©3-9-94 · POB 170515· SF CA 94117

THIS MODERN WORLD by TOM TOMORROW

BILL CLINTON'S MOST POPULAR CAMPAIGN PROMISE WAS TO "END WELFARE AS WE KNOW IT"... PROVING ONCE AGAIN THAT AMERICANS CERTAINLY HAVE THEIR PRIORITIES STRAIGHT!

THAT'S *RIGHT!* AFTER ALL, WELFARE ACCOUNTS FOR A FULL *ONE PERCENT* OF ANNUAL GOVERNMENT SPENDING!

IT'S AN *OUTRAGE!*

OF COURSE, *EVERYONE* KNOWS WHAT THE *REAL* PROBLEM IS...IT'S ALL THOSE TEENAGE *WELFARE MOTHERS* WHO HAVE BABIES JUST TO QUALIFY FOR THE AVERAGE ADDITIONAL PAYMENT OF $67.00...

WHAT A *SCAM!* I'LL BET THEY'RE USING THAT MONEY TO BUY *CADILLACS!*

NO *WONDER* THE DEFICIT IS SO HIGH!

CONSERVATIVES SUCH AS BILL BENNETT HAVE A SOLUTION: TAKE THE CHILDREN AWAY FROM THESE MOMS--AND PUT THEM IN STATE-RUN *ORPHANAGES!*

WAIT...WAIT...AREN'T YOU GUYS THE ONES WHO ARE ALWAYS COMPLAINING ABOUT "LIBERAL SOCIAL ENGINEERING"..?

THIS IS *DIFFERENT!*--ITS *CONSERVATIVE* SOCIAL ENGINEERING!

The Book of Virtues

OF COURSE, IT *IS* POSSIBLE THAT SOME *SMALL* PERCENTAGE OF THESE PREGNANCIES ARE ACTUALLY *UNINTENTIONAL*...AND THAT A LITTLE *SEX EDUCATION* MIGHT BE HELPFUL HERE...

DON'T BE *ABSURD!* THAT WOULD SIMPLY ENCOURAGE *PROMISCUITY!*

YES, LET'S BE *SENSIBLE!*

I THINK WE SHOULD JUST *CRIMINALIZE SEX!*

TOM TOMORROW © 6-29-94

THIS MODERN WORLD

by TOM TOMORROW

THE DEBATE OVER SMOKING *CONTINUES*...LAST WEEK, TOBACCO INDUSTRY EXECUTIVES TESTIFIED BEFORE A HOUSE SUBCOMMITTEE...

WELL, YES...CIGARETTES *DO* CONTAIN SOME *AMMONIA*...A LITTLE *PESTICIDE*...AND A PINCH OF *CHLOROFLOUROCARBONS*...

BUT THEY'RE *PERFECTLY SAFE!*

AND *CERTAINLY* NOT *ADDICTIVE!*

TRUST US!

THEY WERE RAKED OVER THE COALS, AND RIGHT-FULLY SO...STILL, THE EVENT WAS SO HEAVILY *STAGED* IT WAS OFTEN DIFFICULT TO TAKE *EITHER* SIDE SERIOUSLY...

...AND I HAVE HERE A PICTURE OF AN ADORABLE LITTLE PUPPY...WHICH WAS RUN OVER BY A *TOBACCO TRUCK!*

WHAT DO YOU GENTLEMEN HAVE TO SAY ABOUT *THAT?*

IT'S TOO SOON TO KNOW WHERE ALL THIS WILL LEAD...BUT IT SEEMS TO *US* THAT IT WOULD BE A MISTAKE TO *BAN* TOBACCO...AFTER ALL, IT IS NOT THE JOB OF THE GOVERNMENT TO SERVE AS A SURROGATE *PARENT*...

--AND BEFORE YOU GO TO BED, CITIZENS, BE SURE TO *BRUSH YOUR TEETH* AND *WASH BEHIND YOUR EARS!*

REMEMBER, IT'S NOT JUST A GOOD IDEA -- IT'S THE *LAW!*

RATHER, THE QUESTION NEEDS TO BE WHETHER THERE EXISTS AN INALIENABLE RIGHT TO SMOKE IN *PUBLIC*...TO FOUL THE AIR WITH TOXIC FUMES, WITH LITTLE OR NO REGARD FOR ANY-ONE ELSE'S WELL-BEING...

SURE--IT'S IN THE CONSTITU-TION--RIGHT NEXT TO THE INALIENABLE RIGHT TO *DRIVE DRUNK*--AND TO YELL "*FIRE*" IN A *CROWD-ED THEATRE*...

YOU'RE MAK-ING ONE OF YOUR LITTLE *POINTS* HERE, AREN'T YOU, SPARKY?

© TOM TOMORROW 4-28-94...TIP OF THE PEN (GUIN) TO DAVE EGGERS...

15

THIS MODERN WORLD
by TOM TOMORROW

NEWS REPORTS ON THE FINANCIAL MARKETS OFTEN SEEM AS IF THEY ARE BEING BROADCAST IN A FOREIGN LANGUAGE-- OR, PERHAPS MORE ACCURATELY, IN SOME *SECRET CODE*...

--ON WALL STREET TODAY... THE *BLUE CAT* WAITED NERVOUSLY BY THE *LARGE DOOR* IN THE *RAIN.*

NOW THIS...

LATELY THESE REPORTS HAVE BEEN PARTICULARLY SURREAL...BLAMING THE RECENT STOCK MARKET TURMOIL ON A *STRONG ECONOMY* & LOWER *UNEMPLOYMENT RATES*...

--CONDITIONS WHICH MANY AMERICANS MAY HAVE NAIVELY CONSIDERED *DESIRABLE*...

Newsweek
How to Survive in Bear Market

WHY WOULD THE MARKETS PANIC AT SUCH NEWS? WELL, WE MAY BE GOING WAY OUT ON A LIMB HERE...BUT COULD IT BE THAT THE NEEDS OF *WALL STREET* ARE ACTUALLY AT *ODDS* WITH THOSE OF THE *GENERAL POPULATION*... AND *VICE VERSA?*

NONSENSE! HOW COULD TOM TOMORROW EVEN *THINK* SUCH A THING?

HE MUST BE SOME KIND OF UNAMERICAN *KOOK!*

I THINK HE SHOULD BE *DEPORTED!*

THEN AGAIN, MAYBE IT'S ALL JUST BEYOND OUR UNDERSTANDING AS LAYPEOPLE....AND WE SHOULD SIMPLY TRUST THAT COMPETENT, HIGHLY-TRAINED FINANCIAL PROFESSIONALS HAVE EVERYTHING *UNDER CONTROL*...

DUMP A.T.&T!

UNLOAD G.M!

PUT EVERYTHING INTO *POLYSORBATE 80*... AND *TACO SAUCE !!*

CLICK CLICK CLICK CLICK

16

THIS MODERN WORLD by TOM TOMORROW

THIS MODERN WORLD by TOM TOMORROW

Panel 1:
(CONT'D) BILL CLINTON HAS DISCOVERED AN ANCIENT *MASK*...WHICH TRANSFORMS HIM INTO THE PRESIDENT MANY AMERICANS *THOUGHT* THEY WERE VOTING FOR IN '92...

NOBODY GETS OUT OF *THERE* UNTIL WE'VE GOT A COMPREHENSIVE HEALTH CARE REFORM BILL!

Panel 2:
WITH A PREVIOUSLY UNIMAGINABLE SENSE OF *PRINCIPLE*, HE TAKES HIS CASE TO THE AMERICAN PUBLIC...

I BELIEVE A *SINGLE-PAYER* SYSTEM IS THE ONLY REAL SOLUTION--

--AND I WON'T REST 'TIL *EVERYONE* --UH-- *SEES* THINGS MY WAY!

Panel 3:
HE ALSO INFORMS THE MILITARY THAT GAY AMERICANS *WILL* BE UNCONDITIONALLY ALLOWED TO SERVE-- BY ORDER OF THE COMMANDER-IN-CHIEF... AND, USING HIS NEWFOUND POWERS OF PERSUASION, CONVINCES *CLARENCE THOMAS* THAT ANYONE WHO REFUSES TO READ EITHER THE *N.Y. TIMES* OR THE *WASHINGTON POST* DUE TO THEIR "LIBERAL BIASES" REALLY HAS NO BUSINESS ON THE SUPREME COURT-- AND THEN APPOINTS *LANI GUINIER* TO FILL HIS SEAT...

SSSSSMOKIN'!

--BUT NOT *INHALIN'*!

Panel 4:

UNFORTUNATELY HE TAKES THE MASK OFF AT *NIGHT*.

COME HERE, BIG FELLA-- AND BRING YOUR *MASK*!

ALL *RIGHT*!

HEY! WHERE *IS* IT?!

UH OH! CONT'D NEXT WEEK...

TOM TOMORROW © 9-21-94

18

THIS MODERN WORLD by TOM TOMORROW

THIS MODERN WORLD by TOM TOMORROW

THE LAWS OF SUPPLY AND DEMAND DICTATE THAT AS THE JOBLESS RATE *DROPS*, WAGES *INCREASE*... THE FEDERAL RESERVE HAS BEEN TRYING TO FORESTALL THIS BY RAISING INTEREST RATES-- IN AN ATTEMPT TO *SLOW* JOB GROWTH AND MAINTAIN A NICE, HEALTHY UNEMPLOYMENT RATE OF AT LEAST *8 MILLION AMERICANS*...

AND WHERE DID YOU READ *THAT* LAMEBRAIN LEFT-WING CONSPIRACY THEORY?

UM... ON THE FRONT PAGE OF THE *NEW YORK TIMES*, ACTUALLY...

IT IS A RESPONSE TO WALL STREET'S BELIEF THAT RISING WAGES CAUSE *INFLATION*... OF COURSE, IT WOULD BE EQUALLY VALID TO BLAME ESCALATING *PROFIT MARGINS*, BUT THIS IS RARELY MENTIONED...

IT'S ALL A MATTER OF PERSPECTIVE....IS THE CLASS WAR HALF *EMPTY* OR HALF *FULL*?

CLASS WAR? WHAT'S HE *TALKING* ABOUT? THIS IS *AMERICA*!

TWO PERCENT OF THE POPULATION OWNS *HALF* THE STOCKS AND BONDS IN THIS COUNTRY... EIGHTY PERCENT OF AMERICANS DO NOT PLAY THE MARKETS AT *ALL*... AND YET WHEN THE PRIORITIES OF WALL STREET ARE IN CONFLICT WITH THE REST OF THE COUNTRY, GUESS WHO *WINS*...

HEY-- WE'RE THE ONES WHO CREATE THE *JOBS* AROUND HERE, PAL!

AHEM... WITHIN CERTAIN *LIMITS*, OF COURSE...

WALL STREET JOURNAL
UNEMPLOYMENT FALLS TO SEVEN MILLION
INVESTORS WORRY   FED A

IF YOU DOUBT THIS, CONSIDER THAT PRESIDENTIAL ADVISOR LAURA D'ANDREA TYSON RECENTLY ATTEMPTED TO REASSURE THE MARKETS WITH THE NEWS THAT WAGES HAVE BEEN *STAGNANT* FOR SIX MONTHS... WHICH CERTAINLY STRUCK *US* AS AN ODD THING FOR THE ADMINISTRATION TO BE CROWING ABOUT...

GOOD NEWS, DEAR-- I *DIDN'T* GET THE RAISE!

OH HONEY-- THAT'S *WONDERFUL*! THE PRESIDENT'S POLICIES ARE A *SUCCESS*!

TOM TOMORROW ©5-4-94...email: tomorrow@well.com

20

THIS MODERN WORLD by TOM TOMORROW

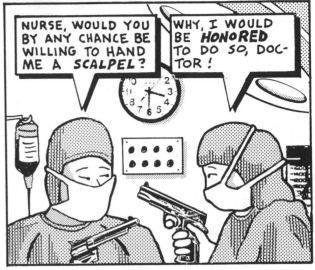

THIS MODERN WORLD
by TOM TOMORROW

RIGHT-WING FUNDAMENTALIST EXTREMISTS HAVE RECENTLY DEVISED A CLEVER *RESPONSE* TO ACCUSATIONS OF *HATE-MONGERING* AND *VENALITY*--

WHY, THAT'S JUST *INTOLERANT CHRISTIAN-BASHING!*

YES! PEOPLE OF FAITH SUCH AS OURSELVES HAVE BECOME A *PERSECUTED MINORITY!*

--ALBEIT A *LUDICROUS* RESPONSE... SINCE THESE ZEALOTS NO MORE REPRESENT CHRISTIANITY AS A WHOLE THAN *WOODY ALLEN* REPRESENTS *FATHERHOOD*...

UH, TOM... "...WOODY ALLEN..."?

WELL, I *WAS* GOING TO SAY "...THAN JOHN WAYNE GACY REPRESENTED *CLOWNS*..."

...BUT IT SEEMED A LITTLE *HARSH*...

ALL FUNDAMENTALISTS ARE NOT VIOLENT WACKOS--BUT A LOT OF VIOLENT WACKOS *DO* SEEM TO BE FUNDAMENTALISTS... AND "LEADERS" LIKE JERRY FALWELL SEEM EAGER TO FAN THE FLAMES OF HATRED...

--AND NOT ONLY THAT--BILL CLINTON IS ALSO THE SECRET HEAD OF THE *GAMBINO CRIME FAMILY!* *AND* HE WAS RESPONSIBLE FOR THE DOWNING OF PAN AM FLIGHT *103!*

(...REV. FALWELL IS APPARENTLY A LITTLE VAGUE ON THE *NINTH* COMMANDMENT...)

NOW THIS CLIMATE OF MADNESS HAS LED TO THE MURDER OF ANOTHER ABORTION PROVIDER... SHOT IN COLD BLOOD BY A MAN WHO QUOTED *SCRIPTURE* TO JUSTIFY HIS DEED...

HEY--HE WAS SIMPLY ACTING ON HIS *RELIGIOUS BELIEFS!*

YES! YOU'RE JUST BEING A *BIGOT!*

THIS MODERN WORLD
by TOM TOMORROW

IF YOU GET ALL YOUR NEWS FROM *RUSH LIMBAUGH*, YOU MIGHT BELIEVE THAT OLIVER NORTH IS AN HONEST MAN WHO ONCE WAS FORCED TO MISLEAD CONGRESS FOR THE *GOOD* OF THE *NATION*...

THAT'S *RIGHT!* AND ANYONE WHO SAYS OTHERWISE IS JUST A *DISGRUNTLED LIBERAL!*

DITTOS

DITTOS

UNFORTUNATELY FOR RUSH, SAYING A THING DOES NOT MAKE IT *TRUE*... IN REALITY, NORTH HAS A LONG AND WELL-DOCUMENTED HISTORY OF PREVARICATION...

--AND THESE ARE JUST A *FEW* OF THE *DISGRUNTLED LIBERALS* WHO ARE SAID TO DISTRUST THE GOOD COLONEL...

Ronald Reagan
Norman Schwarzkopf
George Will
Colin Powell
Alexander Haig
George Schultz
Caspar Weinberger
Ed Meese
Lyn Nofziger
Frank Carlucci
John Singlaub
John Warner

ADDITIONALLY, HE IS A *CRIMINAL* WHOSE CONVICTION WAS ONLY OVERTURNED ON A *TECHNICALITY*... A MAN WHO SUPPLIED ARMS TO TERRORIST NATIONS... WHO SHREDDED DOCUMENTS AND LIED UNDER OATH... AND WHO GENERALLY SEEMED TO BELIEVE HIMSELF *ABOVE* THE *CONSTITUTION*...

--IN SHORT, A *HECK* OF A ROLE MODEL FOR THE LAW-AND-ORDER, FAMILY VALUES CROWD...

Ronal
Norman S
George W
Colin Pow
Alexander

HOWEVER, THOSE WHO ARE ALWAYS WHINING THAT "CHARACTER MATTERS" SEEM WILLING TO OVERLOOK NORTH'S LITTLE *INDISCRETIONS*... OF COURSE, THESE PEOPLE WOULD PROBABLY VOTE FOR *JOHN GOTTI* IF HE SUPPORTED *SCHOOL PRAYER*...

WHY, THAT'S NOT TRUE AT *ALL!*

INDEED NOT! HE'D ALSO HAVE TO OPPOSE *ABORTION* BEFORE HE'D GET *MY* VOTE!

23

THIS MODERN WORLD
by TOM TOMORROW

IN A RECENT "DOONESBURY," GARRY TRUDEAU PRESENTED TWO CARTOON ICONS HE IS CONSIDERING USING TO REPRESENT BILL CLINTON-- AND ASKED READERS TO PICK THEIR *FAVORITE*...

..A *FLIP-PING COIN*...

--OR A *WAFFLE*...

THE PROBLEM FOR US IS THAT *WE* INTRODUCED BILL CLINTON AS *"WAFFLE-MAN"* OVER *SIX MONTHS AGO*...

NOT THAT THAT GIVES US A COPYRIGHT ON *WAFFLES*...

BUT IT *IS* BASICALLY THE SAME JOKE...

THOUGH ON THE OTHER HAND--

OH, SHUT UP.

THE POINT IS THAT WE'RE A SMALL, WEEKLY CARTOON-- WHERAS "DOONESBURY" RUNS IN APPROXIMATELY EIGHTY BILLION PAPERS...

--AND IF TRUDEAU STARTS USING THE *WAFFLE* ICON, WE'LL NEVER BE ABLE TO USE WAFFLE-MAN *AGAIN* WITHOUT BEING SUSPECTED OF *PLAGIARISM*...

MMPH!

...WHICH IS WHY WE'VE BEEN FORCED TO TAKE DRASTIC MEASURES.

NOW LISTEN *CLOSELY*, GARRY. I'VE GOT AN *INDIA INK ERASER* AND I *KNOW HOW TO USE IT*.

MMPH!

CHOOSE THE *COIN* AND NOBODY GETS *HURT*...

MMPH!

THIS MODERN WORLD by TOM TOMORROW

IT IS A **STRANGE POLITICAL SEASON...** FOR INSTANCE, CONSIDER THE INTERVENTION IN HAITI -- WHICH, AMONG OTHER THINGS, HAS GIVEN US THE ODD SPECTACLE OF **ANTI-WAR REPUBLICANS...**

War in Haiti is not profitable for Republicans and other living beings

MAKE MONEY NOT WAR

PHIL

OR TAKE THE DEATH OF **HEALTH CARE REFORM...** THE FINAL NAIL IN THE COFFIN WAS APPARENTLY A REPUBLICAN THREAT TO FILIBUSTER **EVERYTHING** ON THE DEMOCRATIC AGENDA, INCLUDING THE **GENERAL AGREEMENT** ON **TARIFFS** AND **TRADE...**

...AND THEY **CERTAINLY** COULDN'T LET ANYTHING AS INCONSEQUENTIAL AS HEALTH CARE DELAY A **TRADE TREATY...**

IRONICALLY, GATT IS BEING HELD UP ANYWAY -- BY AN OBSTRUCTIONIST **DEMOCRAT...**

AND THEN THERE IS THE CANDIDACY OF **OLIVER NORTH,** RECENTLY ENDORSED AT A FUND-RAISER BY DAN QUAYLE... WHEN ASKED BY REPORTERS WHAT MR. QUAYLE'S SUPPORT **MEANT** TO HIM, THE WOULD-BE PUBLIC SERVANT REPLIED:

ABOUT $50,000!*

*ACTUAL QUOTE.

OF COURSE, ALL OF THESE STORIES WILL SOON FALL BY THE WAYSIDE... AS THE MEDIA DEVOTE THEIR ENERGY TO FEEDING THE NATION'S ALL-CONSUMING CRAVING FOR **MORE NEWS ABOUT O.J...**

DAN, O.J. SIMPSON'S **SNEEZE** THIS AFTERNOON WAS AN INVOLUNTARY REFLEX, POSSIBLY TRIGGERED BY A **DUST MOTE...**

WHAT **KIND** OF DUST MOTE, DAMMIT?! -- I WANT **DETAILS!!**

TOM TOMORROW © 10-12-94

THIS MODERN WORLD by TOM TOMORROW

WE RECENTLY HEARD SOMEONE ON TV COMPLAINING THAT "BEING A SMOKER IN AMERICA IN 1995 IS LIKE BEING A JEW IN GERMANY IN 1938."

HOW DREADFUL IT MUST BE TO HAVE ONE'S ABILITY TO SMOKE TOBACCO IN PUBLIC RESTRICTED.

MY HEART SIMPLY BLEEDS.

IT IS AN ARTICLE OF FAITH ON TALK RADIO THAT WHITE AMERICAN MALES-- POSSIBLY THE SINGLE MOST PRIVILEGED SET OF INDIVIDUALS IN *HISTORY*-- ARE ACTUALLY THE VICTIMS OF UNPRECEDENTED *OPPRESSION*.

HOW DIFFICULT THEIR LIVES MUST BE.

I WONDER HOW THEY FIND THE STRENGTH TO CARRY ON.

WE MAY BE GOING WAY OUT ON A LIMB HERE, BUT IT STRIKES US THAT LATELY, THERE ARE A *LOT* OF RELATIVELY FORTUNATE PEOPLE WHO--HOW SHALL WE SAY THIS?--

--WELL, WHO SEEM TO BE HAVING A WEE BIT OF DIFFICULTY KEEPING THEIR PROBLEMS IN *PERSPECTIVE*--

OW! I STUBBED MY TOE! THIS IS WORSE THAN A SLOW, PAINFUL DEATH FROM *BRAIN CANCER*!

MY BUS IS FIFTEEN MINUTES LATE! THEY DIDN'T HAVE IT THIS BAD ON THE *BATAAN DEATH MARCH*!

THERE'S TOO MUCH STATIC TO LISTEN TO RUSH TODAY! THIS IS MORE TERRIBLE THAN LIFE IN A *STALINIST GULAG*!

--TO PUT IT *POLITELY*...

TOM TOMORROW©3-8-95

THIS MODERN WORLD by TOM TOMORROW

ACROSS THE COUNTRY, REPUBLICAN CANDIDATES WEAR THEIR OBSTRUCTIONIST INTENTIONS AS A BADGE OF *HONOR*... CONSIDER, FOR EXAMPLE, *OLIVER NORTH*, WHOSE CONTEMPT FOR THE BODY HE SEEKS TO JOIN IS *LEGENDARY*...

...AND WHOSE CRIMINAL CONVICTIONS--ONLY OVERTURNED ON *TECHNICALITIES*, REMEMBER--DON'T SEEM TO BOTHER CONSERVATIVES WHO USUALLY CAN'T STOP YAMMERING ABOUT "CHARACTER"...

OR TAKE *MICHAEL HUFFINGTON*--WHO IS, UNIQUELY ENOUGH, RUNNING ON HIS COMPLETE *LACK* OF ACCOMPLISHMENTS...

THAT'S RIGHT--I DIDN'T DO A *DARNED THING* IN THE HOUSE--

--AND I PROMISE NOT TO DO ANYTHING IN THE *SENATE* EITHER!

IT'S A CYNICAL AND DEPRESSING STRATEGY WHICH, OVERALL, SEEMS TO HAVE BEEN CRAFTED FOR EASY COMPREHENSION BY *NEANDERTHALS*...

GOVERNMENT IS *BAD!*

DEMOCRATS ARE *BAD!*

VERY, VERY *BAD!*

ME VOTE *REPUBLICAN!*

MEANWHILE, THAT APPARENT MINORITY OF CITIZENS WHO WOULD LIKE TO SEE THEIR GOVERNMENT ACTUALLY *FUNCTION* HAVE LITTLE CAUSE FOR OPTIMISM... ESPECIALLY WITH MOST DEMOCRATS ATTEMPTING TO BE MORE *REPUBLICAN* THAN THEIR OPPONENTS...

--AND *I* THINK WE SHOULD JUST *BURN* THE CAPITOL *DOWN!*

HEY, HOW ABOUT THOSE *FAMILY VALUES*, ANYWAY?!

27

THIS MODERN WORLD by TOM TOMORROW

OVER THE LAST FEW YEARS, FAR RIGHT EXTREMISTS HAVE WON LOCAL ELECTIONS ACROSS THE COUNTRY BY ORGANIZING AROUND SUCH ISSUES AS *FAMILY VALUES* AND *SCHOOL PRAYER*...

WE'VE GOT TO STOP TH' *LIBERALS!* THEY WANT TO *OUTLAW RELIGION* --AND FORCE US ALL TO BECOME *HOMO-SEXUALS!*

REVEREND FALWELL TOLD US!

POLLING PLACE ←

IT HAS BEEN EASY FOR THEM TO HAVE A DISPROPORTIONATE IMPACT WHEN SO MANY OTHER AMERICANS *DON'T* VOTE-- APPARENTLY PREFERRING TO REMAIN POLITICALLY *ABSTINENT* THAN TO CHOOSE THE LESSER OF TWO ELECTION-DAY *EVILS*...

AAAH--WHAT DIFFERENCE DO *ELECTIONS* MAKE, ANYWAY? =*BURP*=

--*HUFFINGTON & NORTH LOSE BY NARROW MARGINS*--

--*GOP SWEEP*--

--*SINGLE-PAYER DEFEATED IN CALIFORNIA*--

--*PROP 107 PASSES*--

--*GINGRICH TRIUMPHANT*--

BEER

...TO WHICH WE CAN ONLY SAY: *GROW UP*... IN *OUR* EXPERIENCE, MOST OF *ADULT LIFE* CONSISTS OF CHOOSING LESSER EVILS...

HMM... SHOULD I PUT UP WITH THIS *TOOTHACHE* --OR GO TO THE *DENTIST?*

I'M NOT SURE IF I SHOULD PAY THIS *LARGE TAX BILL*-- OR GO TO *FEDERAL PRISON!*

NOT THAT WE MEAN TO ENCOURAGE *COMPLACENCY*, OF COURSE--BUT RATHER THE *OPPOSITE*...THE RIGHT TO *COMPLAIN*, AFTER ALL, IS EARNED BY *VOTING*...

BOY--YOU'D BE IN TROUBLE IF *YOU* COULDN'T COMPLAIN WOULDN'T YOU, TOM?

UM...WHAT'S YOUR *POINT?*

TOM TOMORROW © 11-16-94

28

THIS MODERN WORLD by TOM TOMORROW

Panel 1: BOY, AM I RELIEVED THAT THEY GAVE UP ON *HEALTH CARE!* THE LAST THING WE NEED IS TO LET GOVERNMENT TAKE OVER *ONE-SEVENTH* OF THE *U.S. ECONOMY!*

Panel 2: I CERTAINLY WOULDN'T WANT GOVERNMENT BUREAUCRATS CHOOSING *MY* DOCTOR! AND ANYWAY, WE ALREADY HAVE THE FINEST HEALTH CARE SYSTEM IN THE *WORLD!*

AH, WILBUR--

Panel 3: WILBUR, YOU'RE UNEMPLOYED AND UNINSURED! STOP PARROTING INDUSTRY PROPAGANDA FOR A MOMENT AND *THINK*-- WHAT WILL YOU *DO* IF YOU GET SICK?

OH, THAT'S NO PROBLEM! IT'S LIKE RUSH SAYS-- *NO ONE* GOES WITHOUT HEALTH CARE IN THIS COUNTRY! YOU SEE, ALL YOU HAVE TO DO--

Panel 4: --IS GO TO THE NEAREST *EMERGENCY ROOM!*

WHY, IF YOU GIVE 'EM A FAKE *NAME,* THEY CAN'T EVEN SEND YOU A *BILL!*

OF COURSE. GOSH, I WONDER WHY *HILLARY CLINTON* DIDN'T THINK OF *THAT...*

TOM TOMORROW © 10-19-94

THIS MODERN WORLD

by TOM TOMORROW

PUNDITS *QUICKLY* REACHED A CONSENSUS CONCERNING THE RECENT REPUBLICAN *SWEEP*...

THIS IS *OBVIOUSLY* A REPUDIATION OF BILL CLINTON AND *EVERYTHING HE STANDS FOR!*

YES! IT *CLEARLY* MEANS THAT VOTERS BELIEVE LIBERALS SHOULD BE ROUNDED UP & *IMPRISONED!*

ACTUALLY, WHAT IT *MEANS* IS THAT MOST CITIZENS ELIGIBLE TO VOTE DON'T *BOTHER*-- BUT A SLIGHT MAJORITY OF THOSE WHO *DO* WERE SWAYED BY SIMPLE-MINDED REPUBLICAN *PROPAGANDA* AND *ATTACK ADS*...

CRIME *BAD.*

DEATH PENALTY GOOD.

...AND THERE'S THE *DEPTH* OF YOUR *MANDATE* FOR *CHANGE*...

THE PUNDITS ALSO INSIST THAT DEMOCRATS MUST NOW MOVE TO THE "CENTER"... AS IF THEY HAVEN'T ALREADY BEEN MOVING RIGHTWARD FOR *YEARS*...

THE *REAL* LESSON FOR DEMOCRATS HERE IS THAT IF PEOPLE WANT *REPUBLICANS*...THEY'LL *VOTE* FOR REPUBLICANS! --RIGHT, FOLKS?

TAXES *BAD.*

MILITARY SPENDING GOOD.

IT'S ALL *MOOT*, OF COURSE... THE ELECTIONS ARE OVER... AND NOW IT'S TIME FOR THE REPUBLICAN LEADERSHIP TO FOCUS ON WHAT *REALLY* MATTERS-- THE *1996 PRESIDENTIAL RACE!*

"PRESIDENT *NEWT*"-- HAS A NICE *RING* TO IT, DON'T YOU THINK?

IN YOUR *DREAMS*, DONAHUE-HAIR!

I'M A *SERIOUSE CANDIDAT!* REELY I AM!

TOM TOMORROW©11-23-94

30

THIS MODERN WORLD
by TOM TOMORROW

JUST IN TIME FOR THE HOLIDAYS... IT'S--

The GINGRINCH THAT STOLE CONGRESS!

NO ONE QUITE KNOWS WHY HE ACTS SO VILE; SOME SAY THE GINGRINCH IS JUST FULL OF **BILE**! BUT PERHAPS THE MOST LIKELY REASON OF **ALL**-- IS THAT HIS **CONSCIENCE** IS TWO SIZES TOO **SMALL**!

©11-30-94

BUT IT DOESN'T MATTER **WHY** HE'S THIS WAY, FOR ANGRY HE IS AND ANGRY HE'LL STAY! THE GINGRINCH HATES EVERY DEMOCRAT UNDER THE SUN; WHY, HE HATES ANYONE MORE LIBERAL THAN **ATTILA THE HUN**!

NOW THE VOTERS--IN A MOOD BITTER AND SOUR, HAVE GIVEN THE GINGRINCH **MUCH** TOO MUCH POWER! AND OF **ALL** OF THE PROBLEMS FACING US THIS YULE, HIS FIRST PRIORITY--

--IS PRAYER IN OUR **SCHOOLS**!

NO PROBLEM! **I** WANT THAT **TOO**!

...SAID THE EAGER-TO-PLEASE BILLY-LOU WHO...

TOM TOMORROW (WITH APOLOGIES TO THE LATE, GREAT THEODOR GEISEL)

Note: The following story is one of the earliest versions of *This Modern World* (and is discussed more fully in the Foreword to this book) ...

BILL'S SOON OFF TO WORK, AND JUST LOOK AT THE *SMILE* ON HIS *FACE* AS HE SOARS ABOVE HIS SUBURBAN SECTOR AND INTO THE CITY! HE KNOWS THAT IN THE *PRIMITIVE PAST*, PEOPLE HAD TO WALK THROUGH MILES OF *SNOW* AND *ICE* TO GET TO WORK EACH DAY--AND YOU CAN BET HE'S *MIGHT-EE* GLAD HE WAS BORN INTO *THIS* MODERN WORLD!

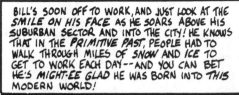

THIS IS EMPLOYEE 434-80-5402 TO IBM CORPLEX--REQUESTING LANDING CLEARANCE! OVER!

BZZT-CRACKLE! ROGER ON THAT REQUEST, 434! VOICEPRINT CONFIRMS IDENTITY! WE ARE LOWER-ING RUNWAY DEFENSES--PLEASE BEGIN APPROACH!

GOOD MORNING, SIR! I WAS JUST WARMING UP THE *AUTOMATIC COMPUTING MACHINES!* SAY-- YOU'RE *EARLY!* AND--IS THAT A *PRESSURE SUIT* YOU'RE WEARING?

YES, IT *IS!* THAT OBSOLETE GROUND CAR OF MINE WAS THE *LAUGHINGSTOCK* OF MY SECTOR! WHY, I'VE HAD IT FOR *WEEKS!* SO LAST NIGHT I WENT OUT AND BOUGHT A BRAND NEW *SUB-ORBITAL CRUISER!* THIS BABY CAN HOP THE OCEAN IN *MINUTES!*

AND SINCE YOU LIVE IN A SECTOR *SEVERAL MILES* FROM THE CITY, THIS WILL MAKE YOUR DAILY COMMUTE *MUCH EASIER!*

YES, THAT'S RIGHT! SO--WHAT'S THE REPORT FROM *SECURITY* THIS MORNING?

YELLOW ALERT, SIR. INTELLIGENCE REPORTS POSSIBLE HOSTILITIES FROM THE BECHTEL CORPLEX!

WELL, I'M SURE THE BOYS IN STRATEGIC DEFENSE WILL HANDLE *THAT!* WHAT ELSE?

A HIGH PROBABILITY OF *LOCALIZED* TEMPORAL-SPATIAL DISCONTINUITIES...

SUDDENLY...

YOU'VE GOT TO BUY--

--AND BUY--

UH OH...

--AND BUY--

--AND BUY!

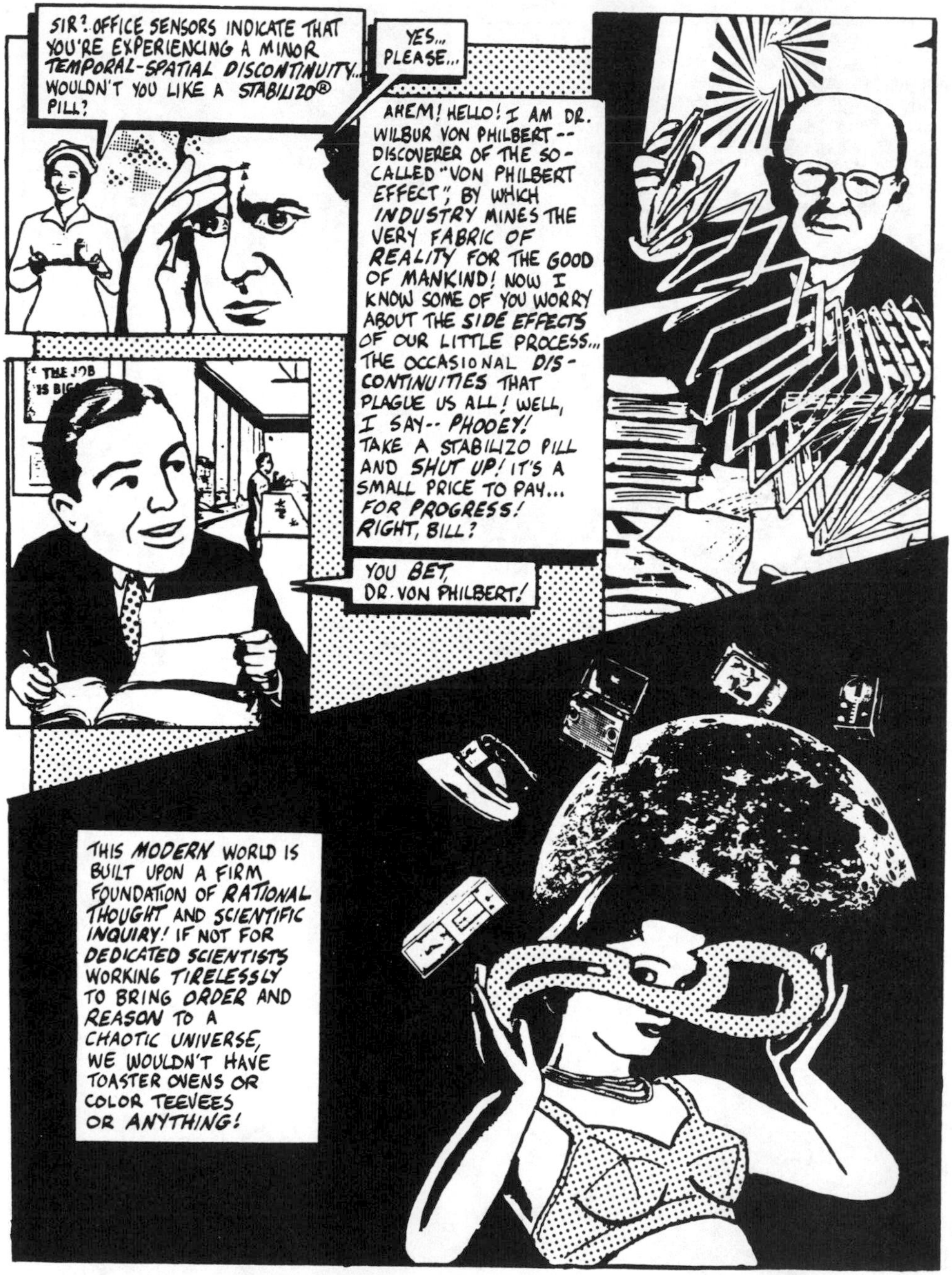
SIR? OFFICE SENSORS INDICATE THAT YOU'RE EXPERIENCING A MINOR TEMPORAL-SPATIAL DISCONTINUITY... WOULDN'T YOU LIKE A STABILIZO® PILL?
YES... PLEASE...
AHEM! HELLO! I AM DR. WILBUR VON PHILBERT -- DISCOVERER OF THE SO-CALLED "VON PHILBERT EFFECT", BY WHICH INDUSTRY MINES THE VERY FABRIC OF REALITY FOR THE GOOD OF MANKIND! NOW I KNOW SOME OF YOU WORRY ABOUT THE SIDE EFFECTS OF OUR LITTLE PROCESS... THE OCCASIONAL DIS-CONTINUITIES THAT PLAGUE US ALL! WELL, I SAY-- PHOOEY! TAKE A STABILIZO PILL AND SHUT UP! IT'S A SMALL PRICE TO PAY... FOR PROGRESS! RIGHT, BILL?
YOU BET, DR. VON PHILBERT!
THIS MODERN WORLD IS BUILT UPON A FIRM FOUNDATION OF RATIONAL THOUGHT AND SCIENTIFIC INQUIRY! IF NOT FOR DEDICATED SCIENTISTS WORKING TIRELESSLY TO BRING ORDER AND REASON TO A CHAOTIC UNIVERSE, WE WOULDN'T HAVE TOASTER OVENS OR COLOR TEEVEES OR ANYTHING!

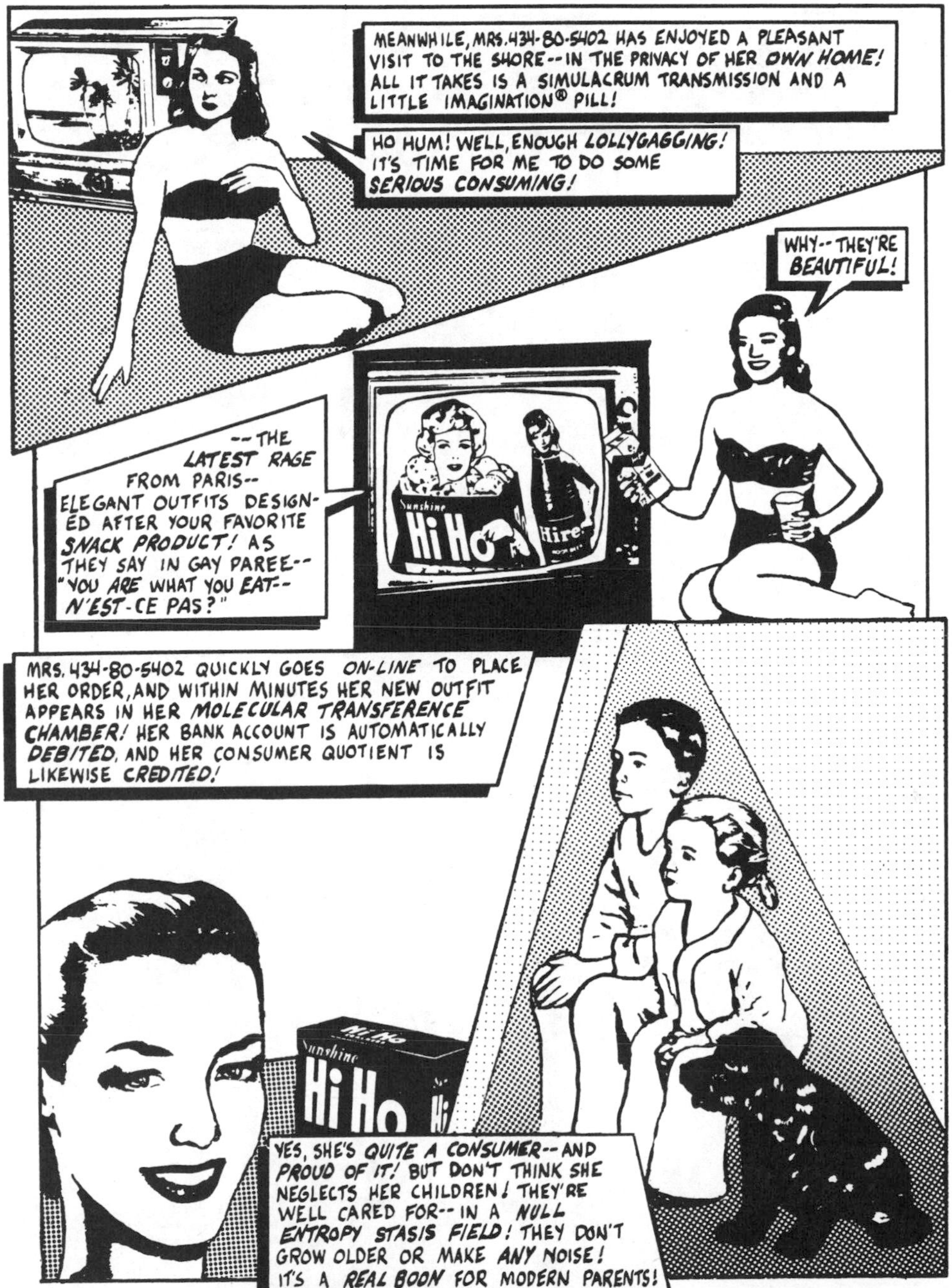
MEANWHILE, MRS. 434-80-5402 HAS ENJOYED A PLEASANT VISIT TO THE SHORE--IN THE PRIVACY OF HER OWN HOME! ALL IT TAKES IS A SIMULACRUM TRANSMISSION AND A LITTLE IMAGINATION® PILL!
HO HUM! WELL, ENOUGH LOLLYGAGGING! IT'S TIME FOR ME TO DO SOME SERIOUS CONSUMING!
WHY--THEY'RE BEAUTIFUL!
--THE LATEST RAGE FROM PARIS--ELEGANT OUTFITS DESIGNED AFTER YOUR FAVORITE SNACK PRODUCT! AS THEY SAY IN GAY PAREE--"YOU ARE WHAT YOU EAT--N'EST-CE PAS?"
Sunshine Hi Ho
Hires
MRS. 434-80-5402 QUICKLY GOES ON-LINE TO PLACE HER ORDER, AND WITHIN MINUTES HER NEW OUTFIT APPEARS IN HER MOLECULAR TRANSFERENCE CHAMBER! HER BANK ACCOUNT IS AUTOMATICALLY DEBITED, AND HER CONSUMER QUOTIENT IS LIKEWISE CREDITED!
Hi Ho
Sunshine Hi Ho
YES, SHE'S QUITE A CONSUMER--AND PROUD OF IT! BUT DON'T THINK SHE NEGLECTS HER CHILDREN! THEY'RE WELL CARED FOR--IN A NULL ENTROPY STASIS FIELD! THEY DON'T GROW OLDER OR MAKE ANY NOISE! IT'S A REAL BOON FOR MODERN PARENTS!

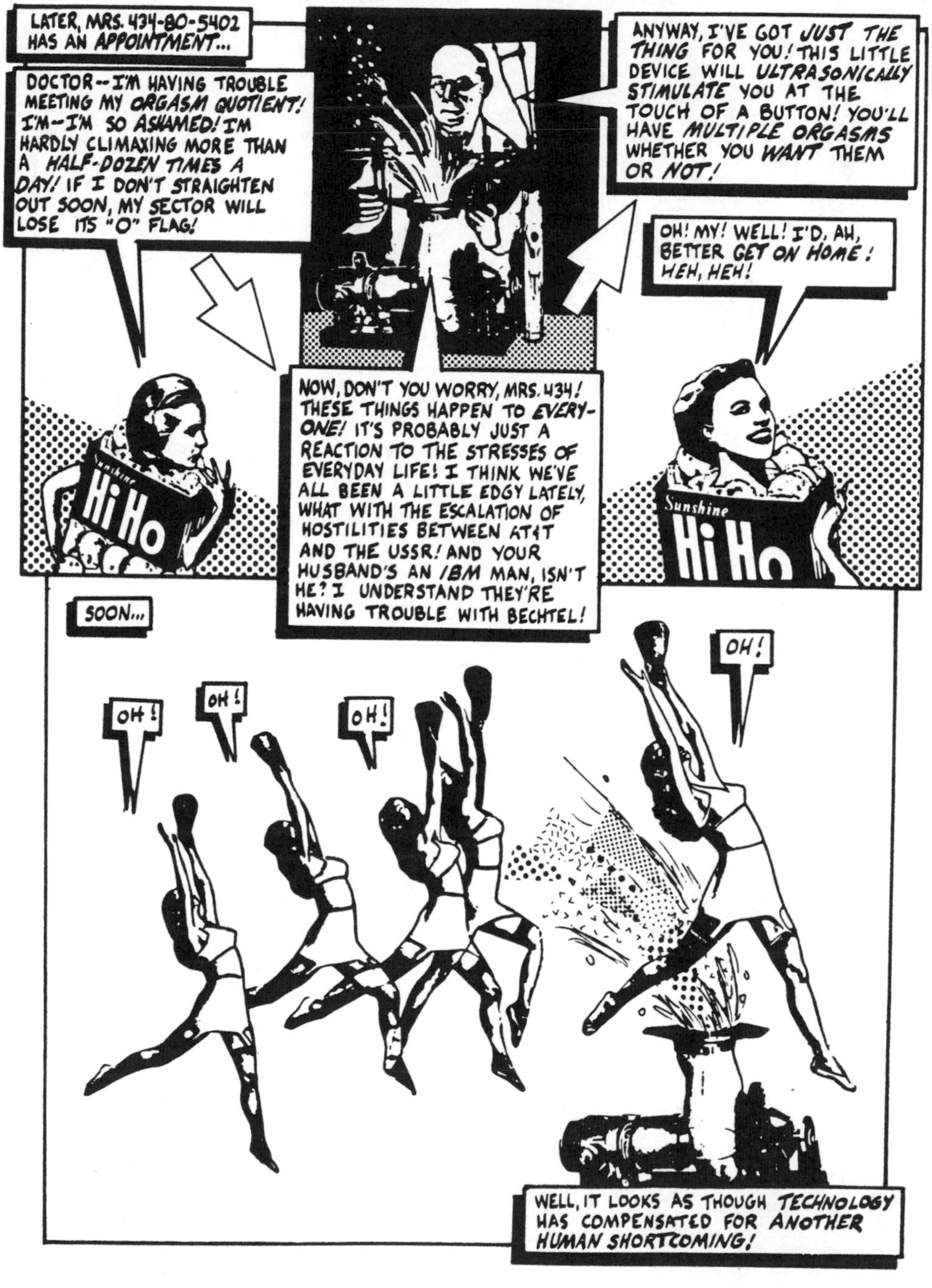
LATER, MRS. 434-80-5402 HAS AN APPOINTMENT...
DOCTOR--I'M HAVING TROUBLE MEETING MY ORGASM QUOTIENT! I'M--I'M SO ASHAMED! I'M HARDLY CLIMAXING MORE THAN A HALF-DOZEN TIMES A DAY! IF I DON'T STRAIGHTEN OUT SOON, MY SECTOR WILL LOSE ITS "O" FLAG!
NOW, DON'T YOU WORRY, MRS. 434! THESE THINGS HAPPEN TO EVERY-ONE! IT'S PROBABLY JUST A REACTION TO THE STRESSES OF EVERYDAY LIFE! I THINK WE'VE ALL BEEN A LITTLE EDGY LATELY, WHAT WITH THE ESCALATION OF HOSTILITIES BETWEEN AT&T AND THE USSR! AND YOUR HUSBAND'S AN IBM MAN, ISN'T HE? I UNDERSTAND THEY'RE HAVING TROUBLE WITH BECHTEL!
ANYWAY, I'VE GOT JUST THE THING FOR YOU! THIS LITTLE DEVICE WILL ULTRASONICALLY STIMULATE YOU AT THE TOUCH OF A BUTTON! YOU'LL HAVE MULTIPLE ORGASMS WHETHER YOU WANT THEM OR NOT!
OH! MY! WELL! I'D, AH, BETTER GET ON HOME! HEH, HEH!
Hi Ho
Sunshine Hi Ho
SOON...
OH!
OH!
OH!
OH!
WELL, IT LOOKS AS THOUGH TECHNOLOGY HAS COMPENSATED FOR ANOTHER HUMAN SHORTCOMING!

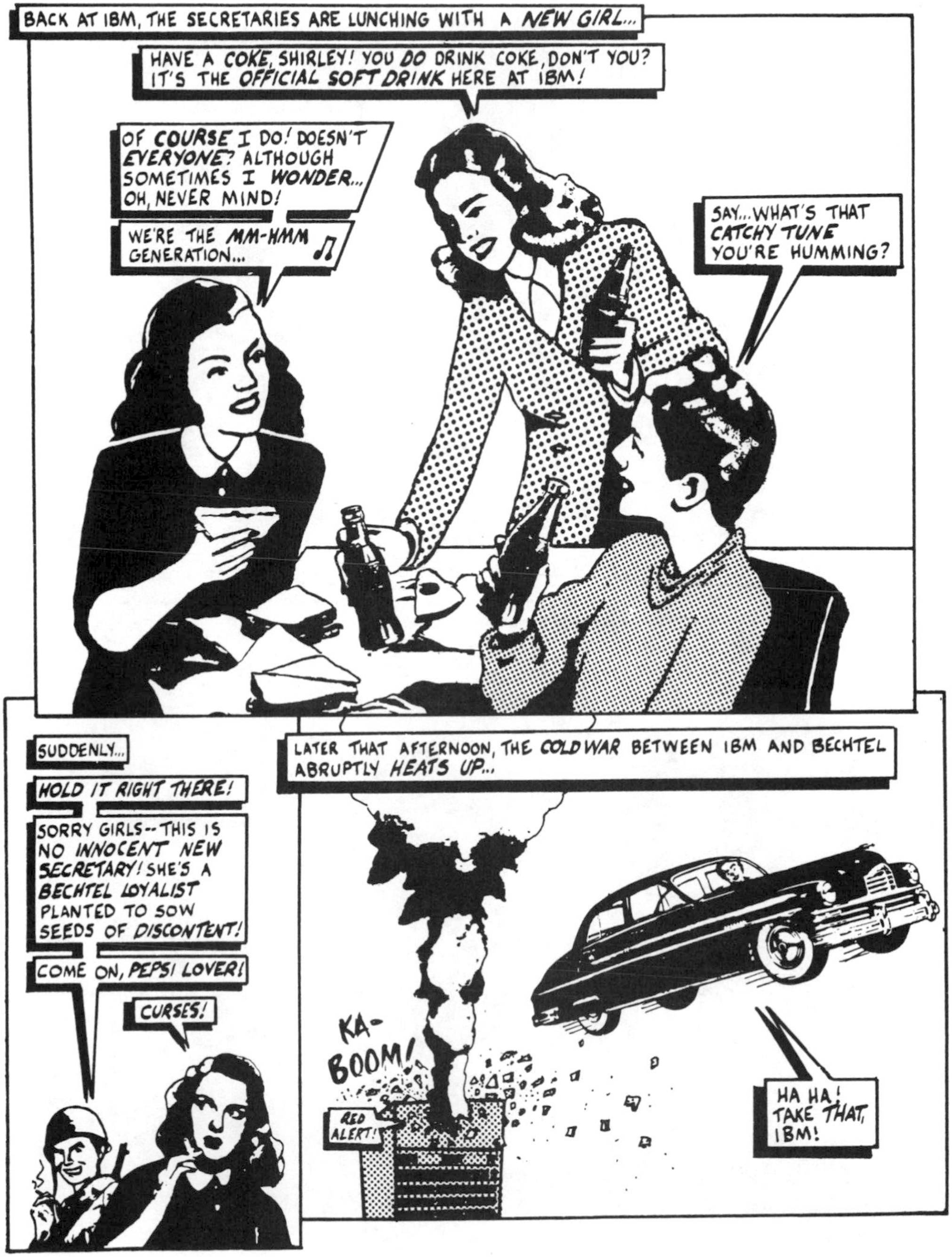

BACK AT IBM, THE SECRETARIES ARE LUNCHING WITH A NEW GIRL...
HAVE A COKE, SHIRLEY! YOU DO DRINK COKE, DON'T YOU? IT'S THE OFFICIAL SOFT DRINK HERE AT IBM!
OF COURSE I DO! DOESN'T EVERYONE? ALTHOUGH SOMETIMES I WONDER... OH, NEVER MIND!
WE'RE THE MM-HMM GENERATION... ♫
SAY... WHAT'S THAT CATCHY TUNE YOU'RE HUMMING?
SUDDENLY...
HOLD IT RIGHT THERE!
SORRY GIRLS--THIS IS NO INNOCENT NEW SECRETARY! SHE'S A BECHTEL LOYALIST PLANTED TO SOW SEEDS OF DISCONTENT!
COME ON, PEPSI LOVER!
CURSES!
LATER THAT AFTERNOON, THE COLD WAR BETWEEN IBM AND BECHTEL ABRUPTLY HEATS UP...
KA-BOOM!
RED ALERT!
HA HA! TAKE THAT, IBM!

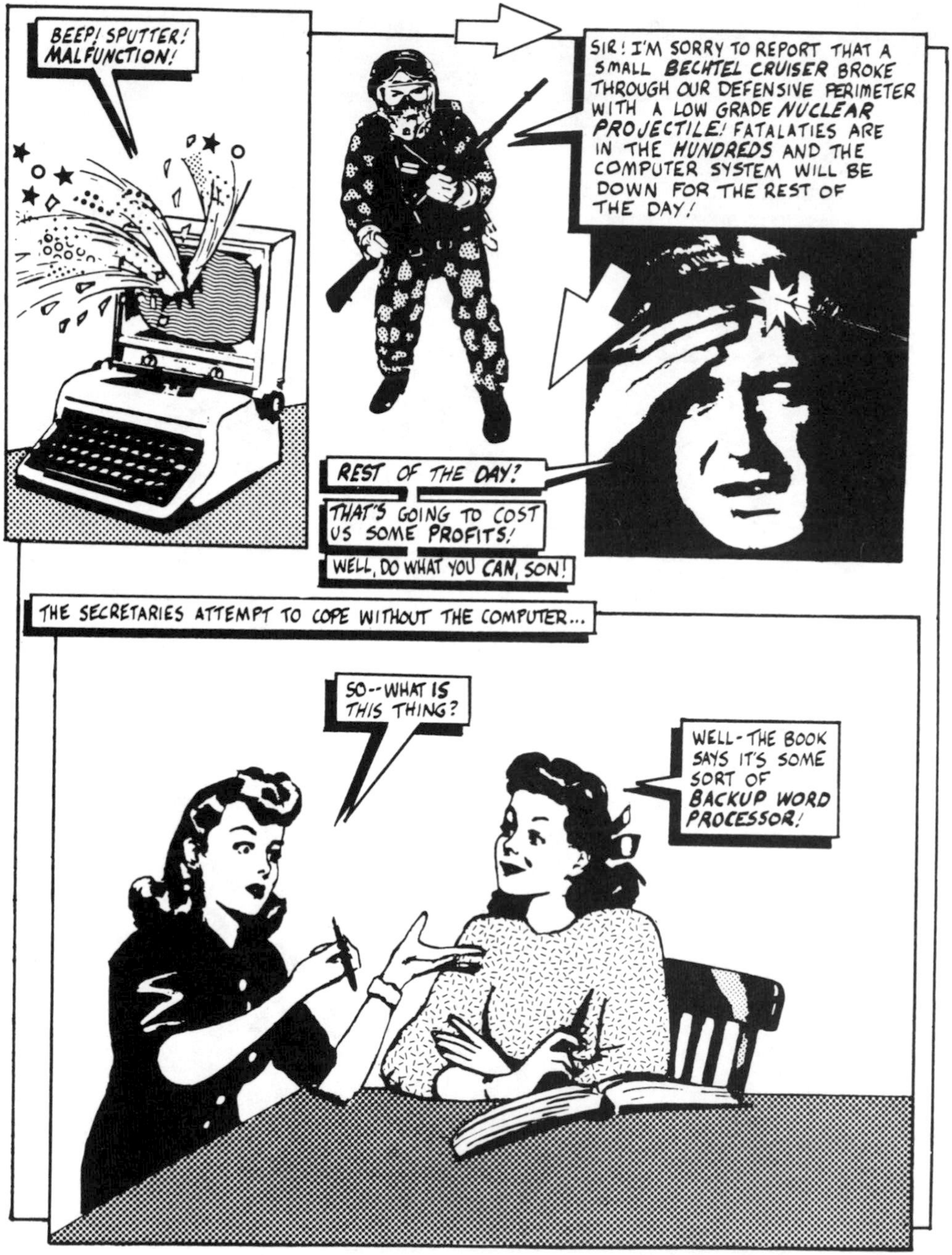
BEEP! SPUTTER! MALFUNCTION!
SIR! I'M SORRY TO REPORT THAT A SMALL BECHTEL CRUISER BROKE THROUGH OUR DEFENSIVE PERIMETER WITH A LOW GRADE NUCLEAR PROJECTILE! FATALATIES ARE IN THE HUNDREDS AND THE COMPUTER SYSTEM WILL BE DOWN FOR THE REST OF THE DAY!
REST OF THE DAY?
THAT'S GOING TO COST US SOME PROFITS!
WELL, DO WHAT YOU CAN, SON!
THE SECRETARIES ATTEMPT TO COPE WITHOUT THE COMPUTER...
SO--WHAT IS THIS THING?
WELL-THE BOOK SAYS IT'S SOME SORT OF BACKUP WORD PROCESSOR!

AFTER THE CONFUSION DIES DOWN, BILL IS CALLED IN FOR A RANDOM *INGESTED SUBSTANCES TEST!*

YES, THAT'S *RIGHT!* AND I'M MORE THAN HAPPY TO SUBMIT TO THE *INCONVENIENCE* AND *DEGRADATION* OF SUCH A TEST IF IT HELPS KEEP MY CORPORATION *STRONG* AND *PROFITABLE!* AFTER ALL, THE *INNOCENT* HAVE NOTHING TO *HIDE!*

THAT'S *TRUE,* BILL! AND IT LOOKS LIKE YOU'RE AS *INNOCENT* AS THEY COME! YOUR LEVELS ARE *WELL* ABOVE MINIMUM STANDARDS FOR INGESTION OF ALCOHOL, CAFFEINE, TOBACCO AND ALL OTHER *REQUIRED SUBSTANCES!*

PRELIMINARY ANALYSIS
SUBJECT: BILL 43480
ALCOHOL: 89%
CAFFEINE: 93%
TOBACCO: 94%
MISC. CARCINOGENS: 86%

THEN BILL HAS A MEETING WITH THE *BOSS!*

QUITE A *DAY,* EH BILL? I MUST SAY, YOU'VE HANDLED IT RATHER WELL. IT'S A RARE MAN THAT CAN TAKE THE KIND OF PRESSURE THAT'S INVOLVED AT THE EXECUTIVE LEVEL, KNOW WHAT I MEAN?

I'VE BEEN KEEPING AN EYE ON YOU, BOY! I THINK YOU'RE GOING TO BE *GOING PLACES!* I'LL BE INTERFACING WITH YOUR HOME MONITOR TONIGHT BUT THAT'S JUST A FORMALITY--I THINK YOU'LL BE MOVING UP THE LADDER *PRETTY SOON!* I THINK YOU'VE GOT WHAT IT TAKES TO DEAL WITH THE STRESS, KEEP A COOL HEAD, AND *NOT BREAK* UNDER THE *STRAIN!*

SAY WHAT DO YOU THINK OF MY LITTLE *EXPERIMENT* IN THE AQUARIUM THERE ON THE WALL? THESE TURTLES TODAY, THEY JUST DON'T UNDERSTAND THE IMPORTANCE OF BEING ON TIME! IT'S NOT LIKE WHEN *WE* WERE TURTLES, IS IT BOY?

YES SIR!

THANK YOU, SIR!

WHEN WE--? AH--AHEM! NO, SIR!

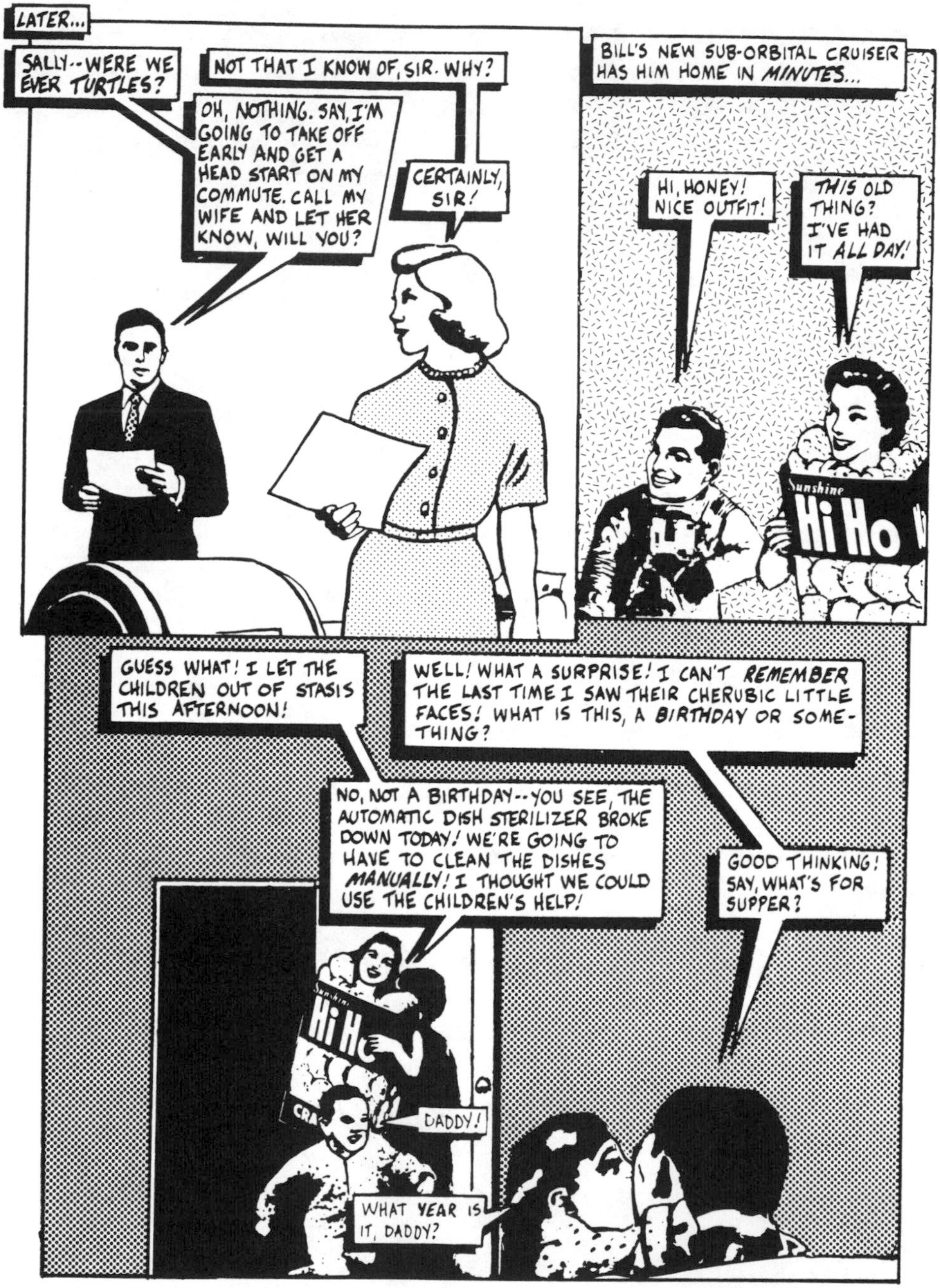
LATER...
SALLY--WERE WE EVER TURTLES?
NOT THAT I KNOW OF, SIR. WHY?
OH, NOTHING. SAY, I'M GOING TO TAKE OFF EARLY AND GET A HEAD START ON MY COMMUTE. CALL MY WIFE AND LET HER KNOW, WILL YOU?
CERTAINLY, SIR!
BILL'S NEW SUB-ORBITAL CRUISER HAS HIM HOME IN MINUTES...
HI, HONEY! NICE OUTFIT!
THIS OLD THING? I'VE HAD IT ALL DAY!
Sunshine
Hi Ho
GUESS WHAT! I LET THE CHILDREN OUT OF STASIS THIS AFTERNOON!
WELL! WHAT A SURPRISE! I CAN'T REMEMBER THE LAST TIME I SAW THEIR CHERUBIC LITTLE FACES! WHAT IS THIS, A BIRTHDAY OR SOME-THING?
NO, NOT A BIRTHDAY--YOU SEE, THE AUTOMATIC DISH STERILIZER BROKE DOWN TODAY! WE'RE GOING TO HAVE TO CLEAN THE DISHES MANUALLY! I THOUGHT WE COULD USE THE CHILDREN'S HELP!
GOOD THINKING! SAY, WHAT'S FOR SUPPER?
DADDY!
WHAT YEAR IS IT, DADDY?

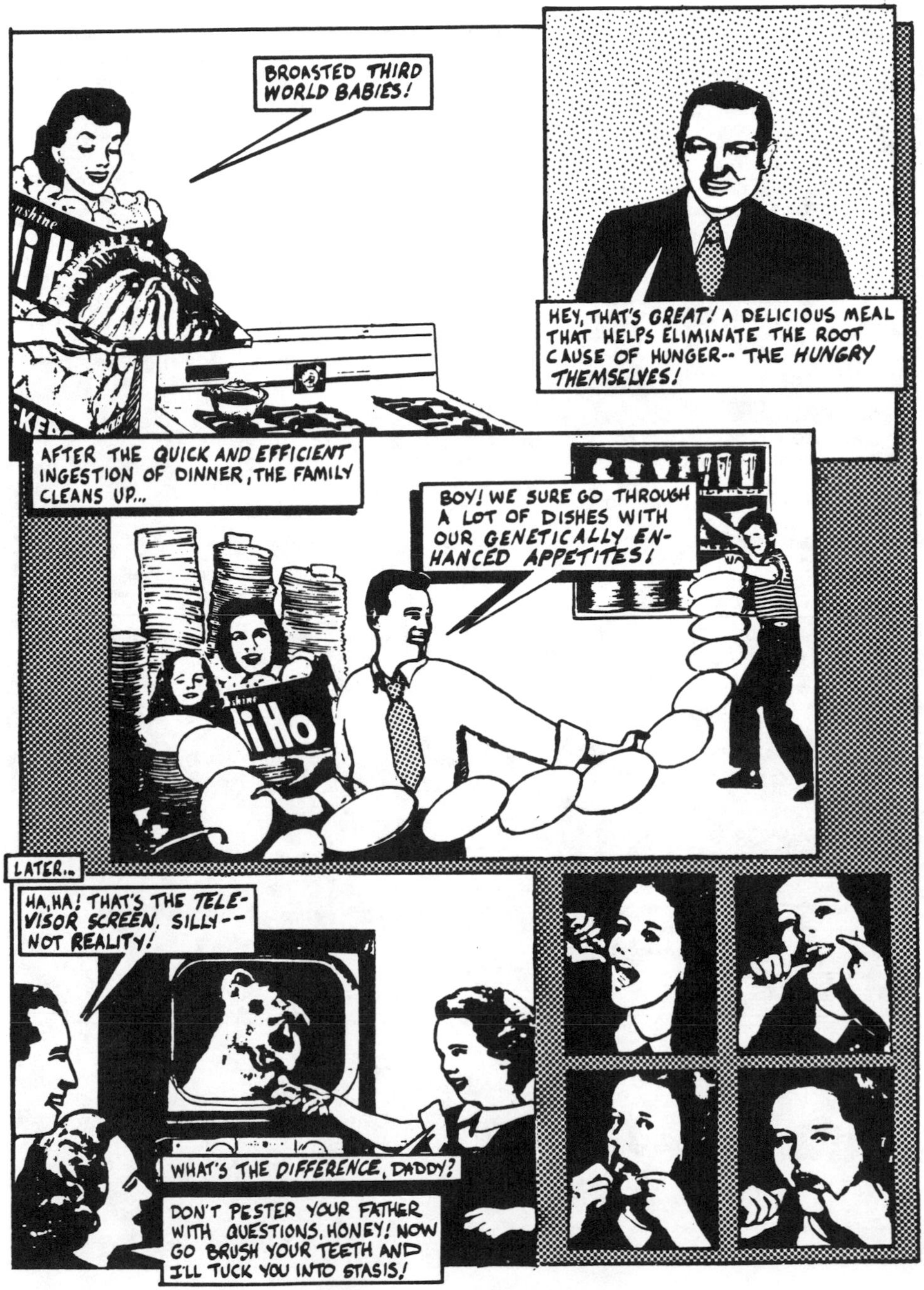
BROASTED THIRD WORLD BABIES!
HEY, THAT'S GREAT! A DELICIOUS MEAL THAT HELPS ELIMINATE THE ROOT CAUSE OF HUNGER-- THE HUNGRY THEMSELVES!
AFTER THE QUICK AND EFFICIENT INGESTION OF DINNER, THE FAMILY CLEANS UP...
BOY! WE SURE GO THROUGH A LOT OF DISHES WITH OUR GENETICALLY ENHANCED APPETITES!
LATER..
HA, HA! THAT'S THE TELEVISOR SCREEN, SILLY-- NOT REALITY!
WHAT'S THE DIFFERENCE, DADDY?
DON'T PESTER YOUR FATHER WITH QUESTIONS, HONEY! NOW GO BRUSH YOUR TEETH AND I'LL TUCK YOU INTO STASIS!

HEY--NOT SO *CAREFULLY!* HOW DO YOU EXPECT TO EVER GET YOUR FIRST SET OF *COMPUTERIZED AUTO-TEETH* IF YOU DON'T LET YOUR REAL ONES WEAR OUT? GO EAT SOME *SUGAR*, OKAY?

YES, MOMMY! I'M SORRY!

LATER, BILL'S BOSS TUNES IN TO THE 434'S MONITOR FOR A *LIFESTYLE INSPECTION...*

HI, BOSS! YOU KNOW--WE FEEL THAT *UNOCCUPIED MINDS* ARE THE *DEVIL'S PLAYGROUND!* WHEN WE KICK BACK IN THE EVENING WITH A VARIETY OF OUR FAVORITE SEDATIVE-ENHANCED BEVERAGES AND SNACK PRODUCTS, WE LIKE TO TURN ON ALL OF OUR INFORMATION PROCESSING UNITS-- *AT ONCE!* WE'VE ONLY GOT A HALF-DOZEN VIDEO MONITORS, BUT THAT NEW STEREO OF OURS CAN HANDLE *FIFTEEN* DIFFERENT SIGNALS WITH *NEGLIGIBLE* FREQUENCY CANCELLATION!

YOU TWO SHOULD BE *PROUD* OF YOUR INFORMATION CONSUMPTION! ONLY IN THIS *MODERN* WORLD IS SUCH A THING POSSIBLE! DO YOU REALIZE THAT SUPPOSEDLY WISE MEN SUCH AS *PLATO* AND *SOCRATES* WOULD HAVE BEEN *COMPLETELY UNABLE* TO COPE WITH MORE THAN *TWO* SIMULTANEOUS INFORMATION INTAKES? HA, HA!

..AND DON'T YOU WORRY ABOUT YOUR SUBSTANDARD VIDEO SET-UP! I'M GOING TO RECOMMEND YOU FOR THAT PROMOTION! YOU'LL BE ABLE TO INCREASE YOUR CONSUMPTION FACTOR *NICELY!*

HA, HA!

THAT'S GREAT, BOSS!

YOU'VE GOT TO BUY--

--AND BUY--

--AND BUY!

Sunshine **Hi Ho**

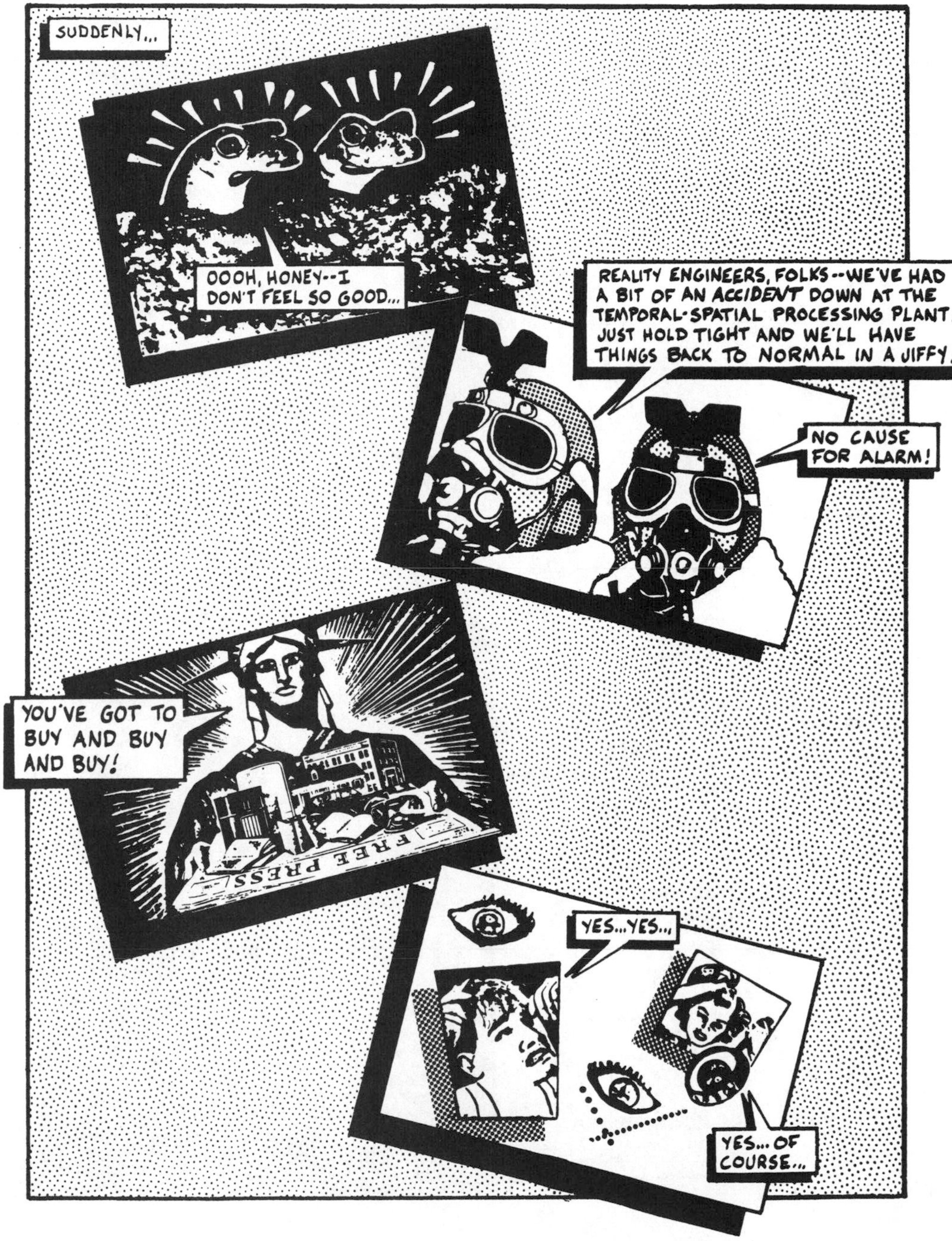
SUDDENLY...
OOOH, HONEY--I DON'T FEEL SO GOOD...
REALITY ENGINEERS, FOLKS--WE'VE HAD A BIT OF AN ACCIDENT DOWN AT THE TEMPORAL-SPATIAL PROCESSING PLANT! JUST HOLD TIGHT AND WE'LL HAVE THINGS BACK TO NORMAL IN A JIFFY!
NO CAUSE FOR ALARM!
YOU'VE GOT TO BUY AND BUY AND BUY!
FREE PRESS
YES...YES...
YES... OF COURSE...

OKAY FOLKS! WE'VE GOT THINGS BACK TO NORMAL, MORE OR LESS! JUST TAKE SOME STABILIZO® PILLS AND RESIDUAL DISCONTINUITIES SHOULD GRADUALLY DIMINISH! SORRY FOR THE INCONVENIENCE!

NO PROBLEM, SON! WE UNDERSTAND THAT THE PROGRESS WE ALL ENJOY IS NOT WITHOUT ITS MINOR PROBLEMS!

GOOD NIGHT, DEAR!

GOOD NIGHT!

THE RESIDUAL EFFECTS DO INDEED DIMINISH... AND AS THEIR COMPUTERIZED WONDERBED® INTRODUCES A POWERFUL TRANQUILIZER INTO THEIR BLOODSTREAMS, THE 434-80-5402'S HAVE A SHORT MOMENT TO REFLECT ON HOW TRULY FORTUNATE THEY ARE TO LIVE IN... "THIS MODERN WORLD"!

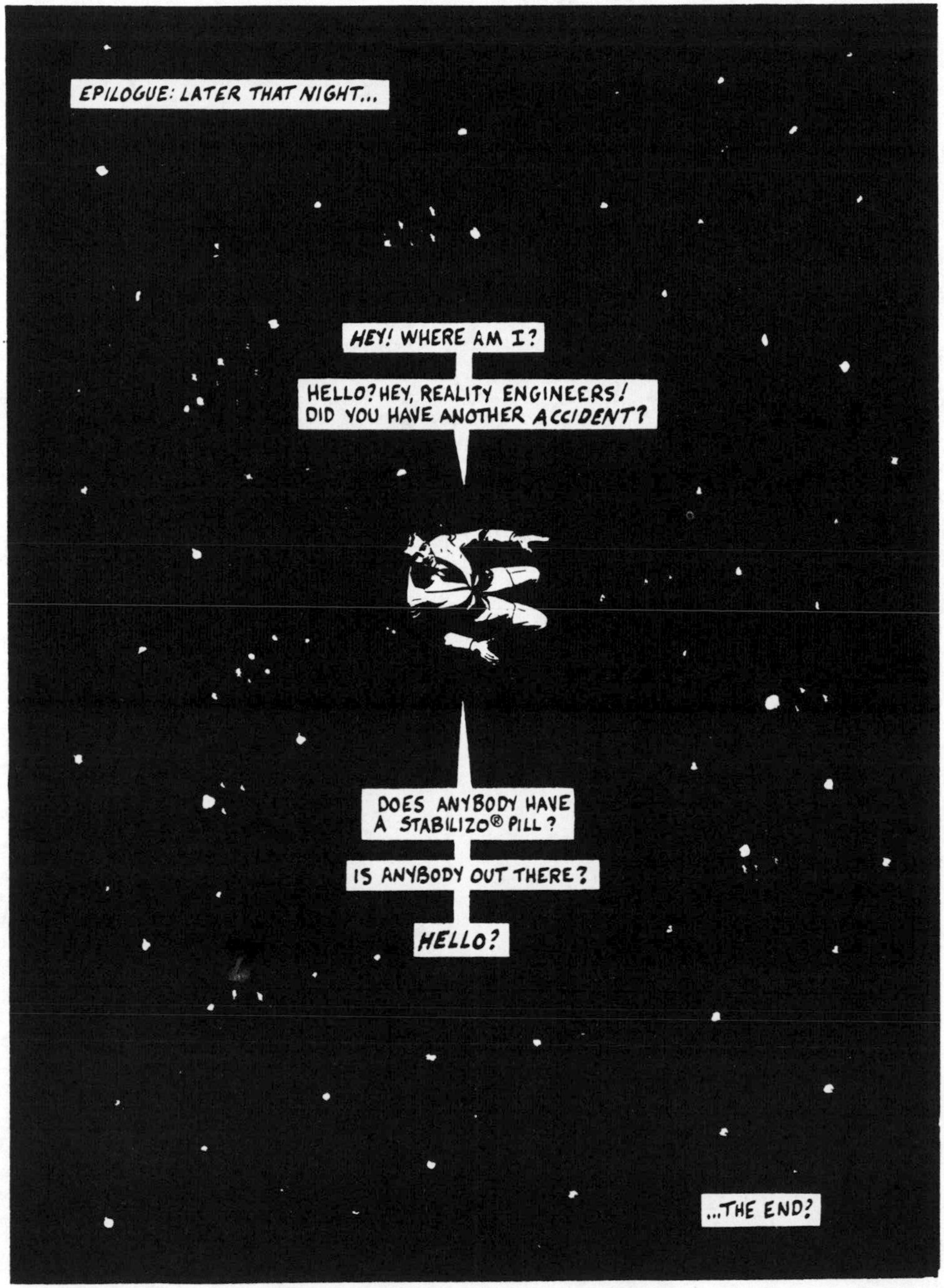
EPILOGUE: LATER THAT NIGHT...
HEY! WHERE AM I?
HELLO? HEY, REALITY ENGINEERS! DID YOU HAVE ANOTHER ACCIDENT?
DOES ANYBODY HAVE A STABILIZO® PILL?
IS ANYBODY OUT THERE?
HELLO?
...THE END?

THIS MODERN WORLD by TOM TOMORROW

THIS MODERN WORLD
by TOM TOMORROW

WELFARE REFORM IS IN THE AIR... WHICH MEANS IT'S TIME TO PLAY WASHINGTON D.C.'S FAVORITE GAME -- *BLAME THE VICTIM!*

SENATOR DOLE -- FOR A SHOT AT THE *PRESIDENCY,* COMPLETE *THIS SENTENCE:* "POVERTY IN AMERICA IS THE FAULT OF..."

"--THE *POOR THEMSELVES!*"

THAT'S *RIGHT!!*

BLAME THE VICTIM!

THE SOLUTION IS SIMPLE, AS FAR AS POLITICIANS ARE CONCERNED -- JUST TELL THE HEADS-OF-HOUSEHOLDS OF AMERICA'S FIVE MILLION WELFARE FAMILIES TO *GET JOBS!* IT'S *THAT EASY!*

OF COURSE, THESE ARE THE SAME GENUISES WHO INITIALLY CONSIDERED FINANCING WELFARE REFORM WITH A TAX ON *WELFARE BENEFITS*...*

*TRUE...

IRONICALLY, THE FEDERAL RESERVE HAS RECENTLY BEEN RAISING INTEREST RATES, IN AN ATTEMPT TO MAINTAIN AN UNEMPLOYMENT RATE OF AT LEAST **6.2%** OF THE LABOR FORCE -- IN ORDER TO "KEEP INFLATION IN CHECK..."

--SO AT THE SAME TIME WELFARE RECIPIENTS ARE BEING VILIFIED AS *PARASITES,* THE FED IS DELIBERATELY *TRYING* TO KEEP A MINIMUM OF EIGHT MILLION AMERICANS *JOBLESS*...

FRANKLY, FOLKS, I DON'T HAVE ANYTHING AMUSING TO *SAY* ABOUT *THAT*...

WHICH IS NOT TO DENY THAT THERE ARE *FREELOADERS* IN THIS SOCIETY... FOR INSTANCE, IF U.S. CORPORATIONS PAID TAXES AT THE SAME RATE THEY DID IN THE 1950'S, TWO-THIRDS OF THE DEFICIT WOULD DISAPPEAR *OVERNIGHT*...

HEY -- THIS IS A DEMOCRACY! IF POOR PEOPLE THINK THE TAX CODE NEEDS TO BE REVISED -- WELL -- THEY'RE PERFECTLY FREE TO HIRE THEIR *OWN* LOBBYISTS!

WE'RE NOT STOPPING THEM!

7-27-94 © TOM TOMORROW, THE WORLD'S MOST VERBOSE CARTOONIST

THIS MODERN WORLD

by TOM TOMORROW

THESE DAYS, *EVERYBODY'S* GOT AN OPINION! WHY, IT'S PRACTICALLY OUR *DUTY AS AMERICANS* TO EXPRESS STRONGLY-HELD BELIEFS ON SUBJECTS ABOUT WHICH WE ARE *COMPLETELY MISINFORMED!*

I'M SICK AND TIRED OF ALL THE *WELFARE MOTHERS* WHO GET *N.E.A. GRANTS* TO BECOME *LIBERAL HOMOSEXUALS!* IT'S AN *OUTRAGE!*

I'M VERY CONCERNED ABOUT THE *CANADIANS!* THEY'RE A BUNCH OF *COMMUNISTS*, YOU KNOW!

AS FAR AS *NEWT GINGRICH* IS CONCERNED, OPINIONS ACTUALLY NEGATE THE NEED FOR *FACTS*... AS HE READILY ADMITS WHEN DISCUSSING HIS PLAN TO "ZERO OUT" PUBLIC BROADCASTING...

"THE LIBERALS HAVE NATIONAL PUBLIC RADIO ALL DAY--AND *WE* HAVE *RUSH!*"

"*RUSH* LIMBAUGH *IS* PUBLIC BROADCASTING!"*

*YES, ACTUAL QUOTES...

BOY--IS THAT NEWT INSIGHTFUL OR *WHAT?* WHY *SHOULD* WE BOTHER SUBSIDIZING AN INFORMATIVE, NON-COMMERCIAL NEWS GATHERING ORGANIZATION LIKE N.P.R.--WHEN WE *COULD* ALL JUST BE LISTENING TO *PARTISAN BOMBAST* AND *VITRIOL?!*

TAXPAYERS WOULD BE SAVED *ONE DOLLAR* A *YEAR!*

I'D FINALLY BE ABLE TO AFFORD ONE OF THOSE "RUSH IS RIGHT" BUMPER STICKERS!

YES, THANK *HEAVEN* NEWT IS THERE TO GUIDE US ALL THROUGH OUR "THIRD WAVE" *INFORMATION-BASED* ECONOMY--AND ON INTO AN *OPINION-BASED* SOCIETY IN WHICH *FACTUAL INFORMATION* IS SIMPLY *IRRELEVANT*...

--AND SO I PROPOSE REPLACING THE ENTIRE STATE DEPARTMENT WITH MY UNCLE FRED--WHO USED TO OWN A *BARBERSHOP!*

I DON'T NEED ANY FANCY-PANTS DIPLOMATS TO TELL *ME* WHAT THEM FOREIGNERS ARE ALL ABOUT!

TOM TOMORROW ©3-22-95

THIS MODERN WORLD by TOM TOMORROW

Panel 1: GOSH, BIFF-- CAN YOU *IMAGINE* WHAT MIGHT HAVE HAPPENED IF THAT HYPOCRITICAL LUNATIC GINGRICH HAD ACTUALLY BECOME SPEAKER OF THE HOUSE?

Panel 2: WELL, THERE WASN'T MUCH CHANCE OF *THAT*... AFTER ALL, PRESIDENT CLINTON'S POPULARITY HAS BEEN AT AN ALL-TIME HIGH SINCE THE PASSAGE OF THE *SINGLE-PAYER HEALTH CARE PLAN!*

Panel 3: I'M GLAD AMERICANS UNDERSTOOD THAT 'SINGLE-PAYER' SIMPLY MEANT A NOT-FOR-PROFIT, PUBLICLY-ACCOUNTABLE *INSURANCE SYSTEM*-- ENSURING *BETTER CARE* FOR *LESS MONEY!*

Panel 4: YES, THE REPUBLICANS REALLY MADE FOOLS OF THEMSELVES, TRYING TO DEMONIZE THIS SENSIBLE SOLUTION AS 'SOCIALIZED MEDICINE'--

Panel 5: --ESPECIALLY ON THE HEELS OF ALL THAT NONSENSE ABOUT THE 'CLINTON TAX HIKES'-- WHICH, AS EVERYONE WAS FULLY AWARE, ONLY AFFECTED A *SMALL PERCENTAGE* OF *UPPER-INCOME CITIZENS!*

WELL, BIFF... BALD-FACED LIES & SIMPLE-MINDED PROPAGANDA WON'T GET YOU ANYWHERE IN *AMERICAN* POLITICS... THE VOTERS ARE JUST *TOO WELL INFORMED!*

MORE FOR YOUR MONEY

Panel 6: IN YOUR *DREAMS*, SPARKY... IN YOUR *DREAMS*...

SAY, WHATEVER HAPPENED TO THAT *RUSH LIMBAUGH* CHARACTER?

OH, HE'S WORKING IN A *McDONALDS* SOMEWHERE...

ZZZZ

TOM TOMORROW © 12-21-94

49

THIS MODERN WORLD
by TOM TOMORROW

THIS MODERN WORLD by TOM TOMORROW

LATELY, SATIRE SEEMS *REDUNDANT*... CONSIDER, FOR EXAMPLE, NEWT GINGRICH'S *LITERARY ASPIRATIONS*...

"I CAN'T WAIT ANY LONGER," HISSED THE POUTING SEX KITTEN. "I MUST HAVE IT *NOW*! I MUST HAVE... A *CAPITAL GAINS TAX CUT*!"

...HIS APPOINTMENT OF A HOUSE HISTORIAN WHO ONCE AXED AN EDUCATIONAL PROGRAM ABOUT THE *HOLOCAUST* BECAUSE IT DIDN'T INCLUDE THE VIEWS OF THE *NAZIS* OR THE *KKK*...

TOO BAD HER APPOINTMENT WAS SCUTTLED BY THE LIBERAL *THOUGHT POLICE*.

THERE'S NO PLEASING THOSE MC-GOVERNIK *ELITISTS*.

...AND, OF COURSE, HIS SUGGESTION THAT LOW-INCOME AMERICANS BE GIVEN *TAX CUTS*-- TO HELP THEM BUY *LAPTOP* COMPUTERS...

HEY, THAT'S *GREAT*! WE CAN STOP WASTING TAX DOLLARS ON FOOD AND RENT SUBSIDIES AND GIVE THE POOR WHAT THEY *REALLY* NEED--

--*INTERNET ACCESS*!!

AND THEN WE HAVE THE *FIRST COUPLE* AND THEIR POST-ELECTION *IMAGE MAKEOVER*...WITH INPUT BEING SOUGHT FROM NEW AGE *SELF-HELP GURUS* AND NEWSPAPER *ADVICE COLUMNISTS*...GOD HELP US...

WE'RE THE *CWINTONS*--

--AND WE *WUV* YOU!

TOM TOMORROW 1-25-95

51

THE TROUBLE WITH BRAINS

Panel 1

MOST OF US WOULD PREFER NOT TO THINK ABOUT OUR OWN BRAINS.

YEAH—IT'S WET AND GRAY AND MUSHY— AND IT'S JUST *SITTING* THERE INSIDE YOUR *HEAD*—

SHUT UP OR I'LL KILL YOU.

Panel 2

TO THE EXTENT THAT WE *DO* THINK ABOUT THEM, HOWEVER, WE WOULD LIKE TO IMAGINE THAT THEY ARE AT OUR *COMMAND*, LIKE OUR ARMS OR LEGS—

—ALL EVIDENCE TO THE *CONTRARY*....

O.K. BRAIN— LET'S FINISH THIS *REPORT*!

Panel 3

FOR INSTANCE, YOU RARELY *CHOOSE* TO GET A TUNE STUCK IN YOUR HEAD— AND YET, YOUR *BRAIN* OFTEN SEEMS TO BELIEVE THAT NOTHING COULD BE MORE DELIGHTFUL THAN LISTENING TO THE SAME INSIPID MELODY FOR *SEVEN STRAIGHT HOURS*....

UM... BRAIN?

"RAINDROPS KEEP FALLING ON MY HEAD...."

GOD, I *LOVE* THAT SONG!

Panel 4

OR MAYBE YOU'VE WASTED HALF A MORNING LOOKING FOR YOUR *KEYS*— BECAUSE YOUR *BRAIN*, APPARENTLY OF ITS OWN VOLITION, DECIDED THAT THEY SHOULD BE STORED WITH THE LEFTOVER *CHINESE FOOD* IN THE BACK OF THE *REFRIGERATOR*....

THEY'LL CERTAINLY BE SAFE *HERE*!

BUY MILK

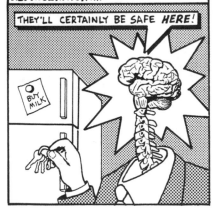

Panel 5

IN SHORT, IT SEEMS LIKELY THAT OUR BRAINS FUNCTION AS *AUTONOMOUSLY* AS OUR *KIDNEYS*...WHICH WOULD AT LEAST EXPLAIN THE COMPLETE *IRRATIONALITY* OF *MOST HUMAN BEHAVIOR*....

I AM REPELLED BY YOU FOR NO APPARENT REASON! CLEARLY WE MUST ENGAGE IN A DEVASTATING WAR THAT WILL RIP OUR RESPECTIVE SOCIETIES ASUNDER!

FINDING YOU EQUALLY DISTASTEFUL, I QUITE CONCUR!

Panel 6

OF COURSE, MANY READERS OF THIS PAGE WILL REJECT THE NOTION THAT THEY ARE ANYTHING LESS THAN THE *CAPTAINS* OF THEIR *VESSELS*...INSISTING THAT THEY *WANT* TO HUM "RAINDROPS KEEP FALLING ON MY HEAD" FOR THE NEXT FEW HOURS....

WELL— IT *IS* A VERY CATCHY SONG!

YES— POIGNANT YET UPLIFTING!

"NOTHIN'S WORRYIN' MEEE...."

HEY! ANYBODY SEEN MY *KEYS*?

TOM TOMORROW ©1995

THIS MODERN WORLD by TOM TOMORROW

Panel 1:

THINGS HAD BEEN GETTING PRETTY ROUGH LATELY, EVEN BY *THIS* TOWN'S STANDARDS ...A NEW MOB HAD MOVED IN & THEY WERE ABOUT AS GENTLE AS A HERD OF ELEPHANTS...IN FACT, THEY *WERE* A HERD OF ELEPHANTS...

THAT WAS FUN! NOW WHUDDYA WANNA DO?

LET'S GO BEAT UP SOME *ELITISTS*!

Panel 2:

THEIR LEADER WAS A SLIMY CHARACTER CALLED THE *NEWT*...FANCIED HIMSELF A MAN OF *ERUDITION*...RUMOR WAS HE'D EVEN *TAUGHT* AT SOME TWO-BIT COW COLLEGE BEFORE GETTING INTO THE *RACKETS*...

...YOU SEE, MEN CAN LIVE IN *DITCHES* EATING *GIRAFFES* -- 'CAUSE WE DON'T GET NO *INFECTIONS*!

GOSH YOU'RE *SMART*, BOSS!

Panel 3:

TROUBLE WAS, THE MOBS IN THIS TOWN ALREADY *HAD* A BOSS...BILLY CEE, BETTER KNOWN AS THE *WAFFLE*...A MAN SO SPINELESS HE GAVE *JELLYFISH* A BAD NAME...

SURE NEWT--I'D BE *HAPPY* TO WASH YOUR CAR!

AND SHINE YOUR SHOES? UH--OKAY! NO *PROBLEM*!

Panel 4:

ME, I WAS JUST A PRIVATE EYE TRYING TO KEEP MY BEAK CLEAN...BUT WHEN THE OLD CODGER CAME THROUGH MY DOOR, I KNEW IT WOULDN'T BE *EASY*...

MR. PENGUIN--THE NEWT SAYS HE'S GOT A *CONTRACT* WITH ME--BUT I NEVER *SIGNED* A *THING*!

I NEED *YOUR* HELP!

HE PAID MY FEE WITH A *CREDIT CARD*... SAID HE WAS HAVING *DEFICIT* PROBLEMS...(CONT'D NEXT WEEK!)

THIS MODERN WORLD

by TOM TOMORROW

(CONT'D) I'D BEEN HIRED BY A GEEZER WITH STRANGE TASTE IN CLOTHES... A MOBSTER CALLED THE *NEWT* WAS TRYING TO ENFORCE SOME *CONTRACT* THE OLD MAN HAD NEVER *SIGNED*...

I NEED YOUR HELP!

I TRACKED DOWN ONE OF THE NEWT'S MOST FAWNING LACKEYS--A LOUD-MOUTHED DEEJAY WHO'D ALWAYS SOUNDED TO ME LIKE HIS *NEEDLE* WAS *STUCK*...

WHAT--WHAT--I MEAN--I'LL TELLYA--YOU LIBERALS--WHY--WHY--I MEAN--I--I--

JUST GIVE HIM THE *MESSAGE*, RADIO BOY.

ON AIR

IT DIDN'T TAKE LONG FOR A COUPLE OF GOONS TO PAY ME A VISIT.

TIME TO GO FOR A *RIDE*, PENGUIN.

YOU BOYS HAVE BEEN TAKING A *LOT* OF PEOPLE FOR A RIDE LATELY, HAVEN'T YOU?

IT WAS A SHORT TRIP...THEY MADE SURE I DIDN'T HAVE ANY CONCEALED *WEAPONS* OR DANGEROUS *ART*, AND THEN SHOVED ME INTO THE NEWT'S *OFFICE*...

WHERE I COME FROM, A CONTRACT ISN'T VALID UNLESS IT'S SIGNED BY *BOTH PARTIES*, NEWT.

WELL, WE'RE PLAYIN' BY *MY* RULES NOW! YOU KNOW *WHY*?-- 'CAUSE I'M DA *SMARTEST GUY* IN DIS *TOWN*! WHY, I EVEN WRITE *BOOKS*!

THIS WASN'T GOING TO GET ME ANYWHERE... BUT WHEN I TURNED TO LEAVE I FELT *COLD STEEL* IN MY BACK...

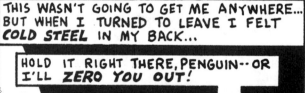

HOLD IT RIGHT THERE, PENGUIN-- OR I'LL *ZERO YOU OUT*!

I AIN'T DONE *TALKIN'* ABOUT MYSELF YET!

HE LECTURED ME ON THE TOPIC OF HIS OWN *BRILLIANCE* FOR A COUPLE OF *HOURS*...IT MIGHT HAVE BEEN LESS PAINFUL JUST TO LET HIM *SHOOT* ME...(MORE NEXT WEEK!)

TOM TOMORROW © 2-22-95

THIS MODERN WORLD

by TOM TOMORROW

THIS MODERN WORLD

by TOM TOMORROW

EXPERTS CLAIM THAT WORKING IN SEALED OFFICE BUILDINGS WITH INADEQUATE OR CONTAMINATED AIR CIRCULATION MAY CAUSE HEADACHES, DIZZINESS, NAUSEA, RESPIRATORY INFECTIONS, AND A VARIETY OF OTHER AILMENTS.

WE AT THE *SUPER GIANT CONGLOMERATED CORPORATION* ARE VERY *CONCERNED* ABOUT THIS SO-CALLED "SICK BUILDING SYNDROME"!

WE RECOGNIZE THE POTENTIAL *SERIOUSNESS* OF THIS PROBLEM -- AND THE NECESSITY FOR *IMMEDIATE ACTION*!

THAT'S WHY WE'VE WASTED *NO TIME* HIRING OUR *OWN EXPERT* TO *DISPUTE THE FACTS*!

MY FINDINGS INDICATE THAT THESE SYMPTOMS ARE CAUSED BY *FRESH AIR* AND *SUNSHINE*!

WELL, YOU DIDN'T THINK WE WERE GOING TO ADMIT *LIABILITY*, DID YOU?

56

THIS MODERN WORLD by TOM TOMORROW

Panel 1:

THERE IS MORE INFORMATION AVAILABLE TO AVERAGE CITIZENS TODAY THAN AT ANY POINT IN *HISTORY*... BUT DO THEY REALLY *CARE*?

BOY--AFTER A HARD DAY AT WORK, THERE'S NOTHING *I'D* RATHER DO THAN LOG ON TO THE *NEW CONGRESSIONAL INTERNET SITE*!

EXCEPT MAYBE SHOVE LARGE SPIKES INTO MY EYEBALLS.

Panel 2:

THERE ACTUALLY SEEMS TO BE A GROWING *BACKLASH* TO THE INFORMATION AGE... STUPIDITY AND IGNORANCE ARE BEING CELEBRATED EVERYWHERE IN POPULAR CULTURE, FROM MOVIES TO MTV... NOT TO *MENTION* TALK RADIO...

HEY RUSH--I GET *ALL* MY NEWS FROM *YOU!* HUH HUH! HUH HUH!

A *WISE CHOICE*, YOUNG MAN! LEMME TELLYA--THE LIBERAL MEDIA--SPLUTTER--SPLUTTER--

HUH HUH!

Panel 3:

ANY OVERLY-ABUNDANT COMMODITY BECOMES DEVALUED--AND APPARENTLY *INFORMATION* IS NO *EXCEPTION*...

CONSIDER THAT IN THE 1850's, AUDIENCES ATTENDED DEBATES BETWEEN ABRAHAM LINCOLN & STEPHEN DOUGLAS WHICH LASTED UP TO *SEVEN HOURS*...

AS NEIL POSTMAN ASKS--WHAT KIND OF PEOPLE *WERE* THESE?

Panel 4:

TODAY, SUCH DEBATES *MIGHT* HOLD THE PUBLIC'S ATTENTION FOR AN HOUR-- AND ONLY THEN IF *HIGHLY ENTERTAINING QUESTIONS* WERE ASKED...

PRESIDENT CLINTON--DO YOU *REALLY* FEEL THAT *JOCKEY BRIEFS* ARE AN APPROPRIATE CHOICE OF UNDERWEAR FOR A *WORLD LEADER*?

IS IT TIME FOR BEAVIS & BUTTHEAD YET?

TOM TOMORROW © 2-1-95

57

THIS MODERN WORLD by TOM TOMORROW

Panel 1: POOR NEWT GINGRICH! THE UNSCRUPULOUS LIBERAL MEDIA HAVE BEEN SUBJECTING HIM TO A CERTAIN DEGREE OF *FACTUAL SCRUTINY*--AND HE DOESN'T *LIKE* IT!

WAAAH! THEY'RE *PICKIN'* ON ME! ≷SNIFF≷ WHY CAN'T THEY JUST SAY WHAT I *TELL* 'EM TO SAY--LIKE ABOUT THE Mc-GOVERNIK DRUGGIES IN TH' WHITE HOUSE AN' STUFF!

GOP

Panel 2: POOR DICK ARMEY! ONE LITTLE HOMOPHOBIC REMARK AND THE BLEEDING HEARTS IN THE PRESS WON'T SHUT *UP* ABOUT IT!

WAAAAH! I DIDN'T *MEAN* TO SAY IT-- IN *PUBLIC* ANYWAY! ≷SNIFF≷ NOW THE NASTY LIB'RULS WON'T LEAVE ME *ALONE*!

STOP WHINING AND GO TO SLEEP.

Panel 3: LIFE IS CERTAINLY DIFFICULT FOR REPUBLICANS! THOSE BIASED REPORTERS SIMPLY *REFUSE* TO TREAT THEM WITH THE MINDLESS, UNCRITICAL ADULATION THEY CONSIDER THEIR DUE!

HEY--THE MEDIA NEVER TREATED *BILL CLINTON* LIKE THIS! WHY, EXCEPT FOR WHITEWATER, TRAVELGATE, HAIRCUTGATE, ALLEGATIONS OF ADULTERY AND ENDLESS COMMENTARY ON HIS LACK OF CHARACTER--

--HE'S PRACTICALLY HAD A *FREE RIDE*!

Panel 4: YES, IT'S *MIGHTY UNFAIR*... AND FRANKLY, WE'D JUST *HATE* FOR OUR CONSERVATIVE FRIENDS TO FEEL *OPPRESSED* OR *VICTIMIZED* IN ANY WAY...

PERHAPS WE SHOULD *LEGISLATE* SOME SORT OF *AFFIRMATIVE ACTION*-- TO ENSURE THAT REPUBLICANS ARE NOT *DISEMPOWERED*!

YOU'RE TRYING TO MAKE ONE OF YOUR LITTLE *POINTS*, AREN'T YOU?

TOM TOMORROW © 2-8-95

THIS MODERN WORLD

by TOM TOMORROW

GREAT NEWS, FOLKS! "TOM'S WORLD"--A ZANY SIT-COM LOOSELY BASED ON *THIS CARTOON*--WILL PREMIERE ON A *MAJOR NETWORK* THIS FALL... WITH *ROBERT URICH* AS *TOM* AND *GARY COLEMAN* AS *SPARKY THE WONDER PENGUIN!*

HEY TOM--I'VE BEEN THINKING...

UH OH! *THAT* USUALLY SPELLS TROUBLE! SAY--

--HOW 'BOUT SOME MORE COFFEE?!

SOON TO BE THE CATCHPHRASE OF THE NINETIES!

HA

HA HA HA

HA HA

HA HA

"TOM'S WORLD" WILL TACKLE CONTROVERSIAL TOPICS *HEAD ON*--WHETHER THE *SPONSORS* LIKE IT OR *NOT!*

SO WHAT'S ON YOUR *MIND*, LI'L FELLA?

WELL--I THINK SOME POLITICIANS MAKE PROMISES THEY DON'T PLAN TO *KEEP*--JUST TO GET *ELECTED!*

MAYBE *SO*, SPARKSTER--BUT YOU JUST CAN'T LET A FEW *BAD APPLES* SPOIL YOUR FAITH IN OUR *DEMOCRACY!* (MEANINGFUL PAUSE...)

YOO HOO-- ANYONE *HOME?*

VERSATILE TV ACTRESS *HEATHER LOCKLEAR* WILL GUEST-STAR AS TOM'S WACKY *CONSERVATIVE NEIGHBOR!*

TOM, I KNOW HOW HARD YOU WORK ON THOSE LEFT-WING, TREE-HUGGING, SO-CALLED "*CARTOONS*" OF YOURS--

--SO I BROUGHT YOU OVER SOME *DINNER!*

AWWWWWWW

DITTOS USH!

HEARTWARMING EPIPHANIES AT THE END OF EACH EPISODE WILL MAKE "TOM'S WORLD" MUST VIEWING FOR THE *ENTIRE FAMILY!*

GOSH, TOM--WHEN YOU GET RIGHT DOWN TO IT, POLITICS JUST AREN'T THAT *IMPORTANT*, ARE THEY?

NOW YOU'RE LEARNIN', SHORT STUFF! SAY, YOU TWO--

HOW 'BOUT SOME MORE COFFEE?!

CLAP CLAP CLAP CLAP CLAP

TOM TOMORROW © 3-29-95 · HAPPY APRIL FIRST!

59

HEY KIDS! NOW YOU CAN MAKE YOUR OWN MODEL OF *SPARKY* IN HIS *NASH METROPOLITAN*!

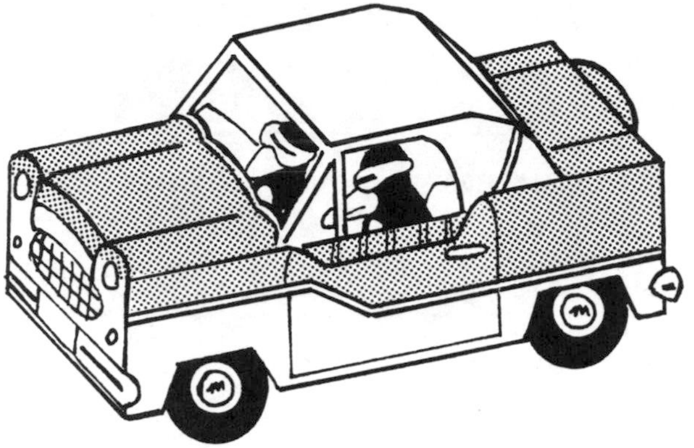

IT'S ***EASY***! JUST COPY THE FOLLOWING PAGES ONTO CARDSTOCK -- CUT THE PIECES OUT, SCORING AND FOLDING ALONG THE DOTTED LINES -- INSERT THE TABS INTO THE APPROPRIATE SLOTS -- GLUE AND TAPE AS NECESSARY -- AND PROCEED TO HAVE ***AS MUCH FUN AS YOU CAN POSSIBLY STAND*** ACTING OUT YOUR ***OWN*** "THIS MODERN WORLD" CARTOON ADVENTURES AT HOME! (EXAMPLE BELOW...)

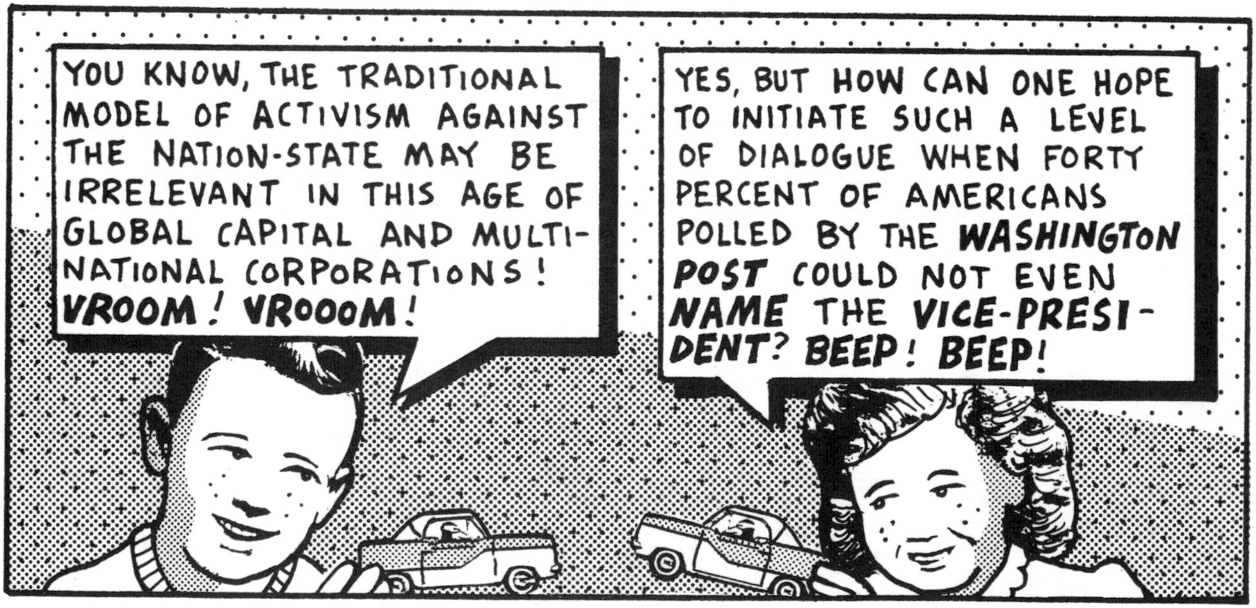
YOU KNOW, THE TRADITIONAL MODEL OF ACTIVISM AGAINST THE NATION-STATE MAY BE IRRELEVANT IN THIS AGE OF GLOBAL CAPITAL AND MULTI-NATIONAL CORPORATIONS! VROOM! VROOOM!
YES, BUT HOW CAN ONE HOPE TO INITIATE SUCH A LEVEL OF DIALOGUE WHEN FORTY PERCENT OF AMERICANS POLLED BY THE WASHINGTON POST COULD NOT EVEN NAME THE VICE-PRESI-DENT? BEEP! BEEP!

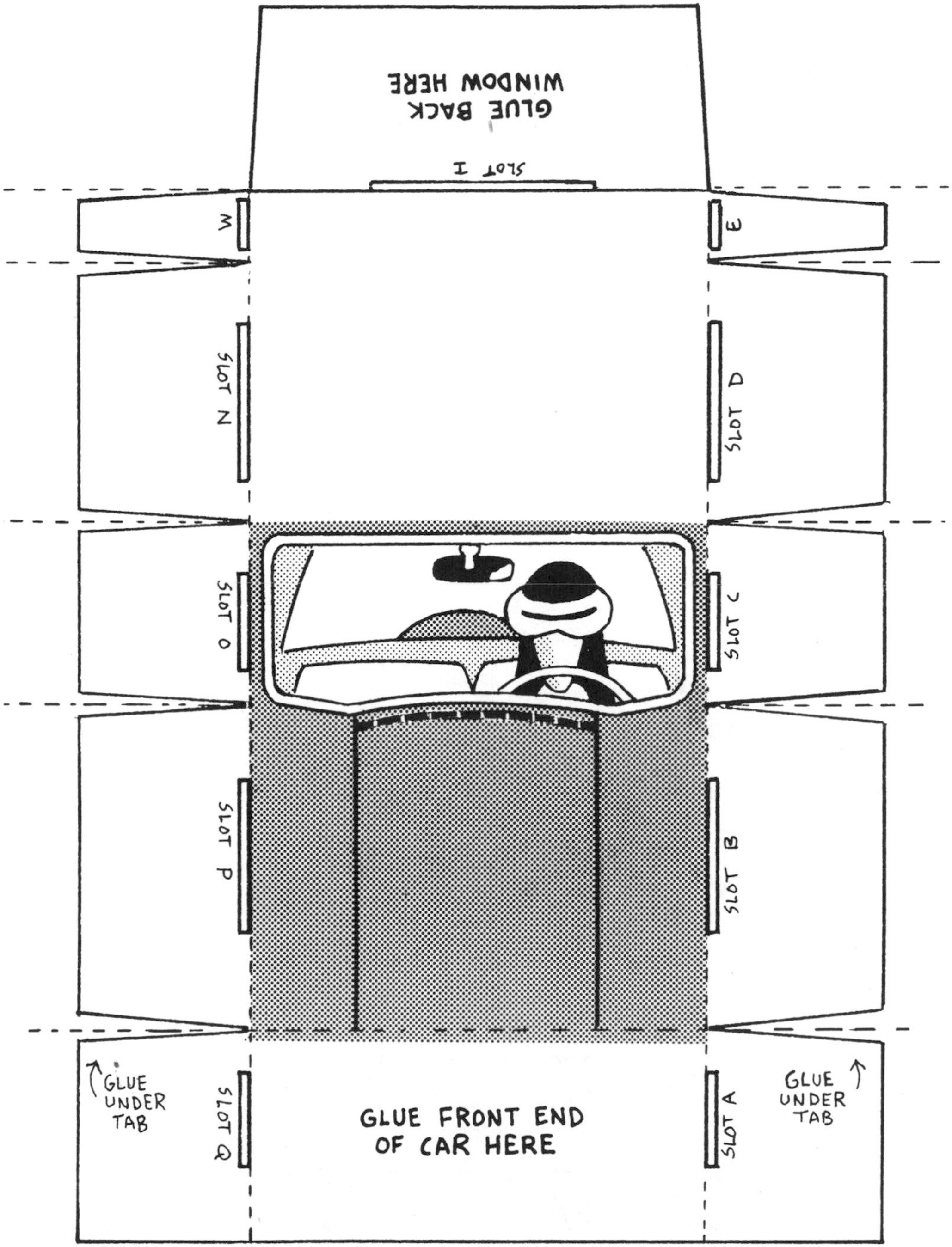
GLUE BACK WINDOW HERE
SLOT I
M
E
SLOT N
SLOT D
SLOT O
SLOT C
SLOT P
SLOT B
GLUE UNDER TAB
SLOT Q
GLUE FRONT END OF CAR HERE
SLOT A
GLUE UNDER TAB

CALIFORNIA
SPARKY

CALIFORNIA
SPARKY

TAB I
SLOT F
SLOT L
SLOT G
SLOT K
SLOT H
SLOT J
GLUE BACK END
OF CAR HERE

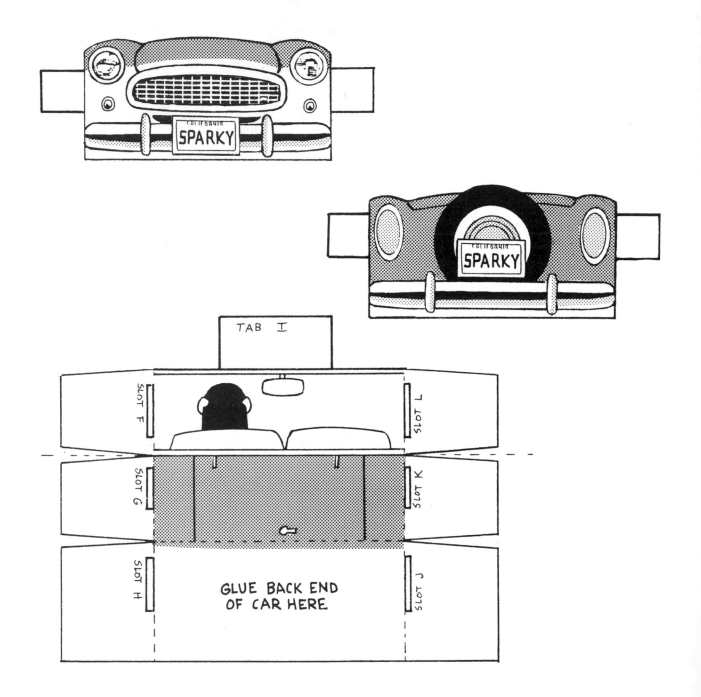

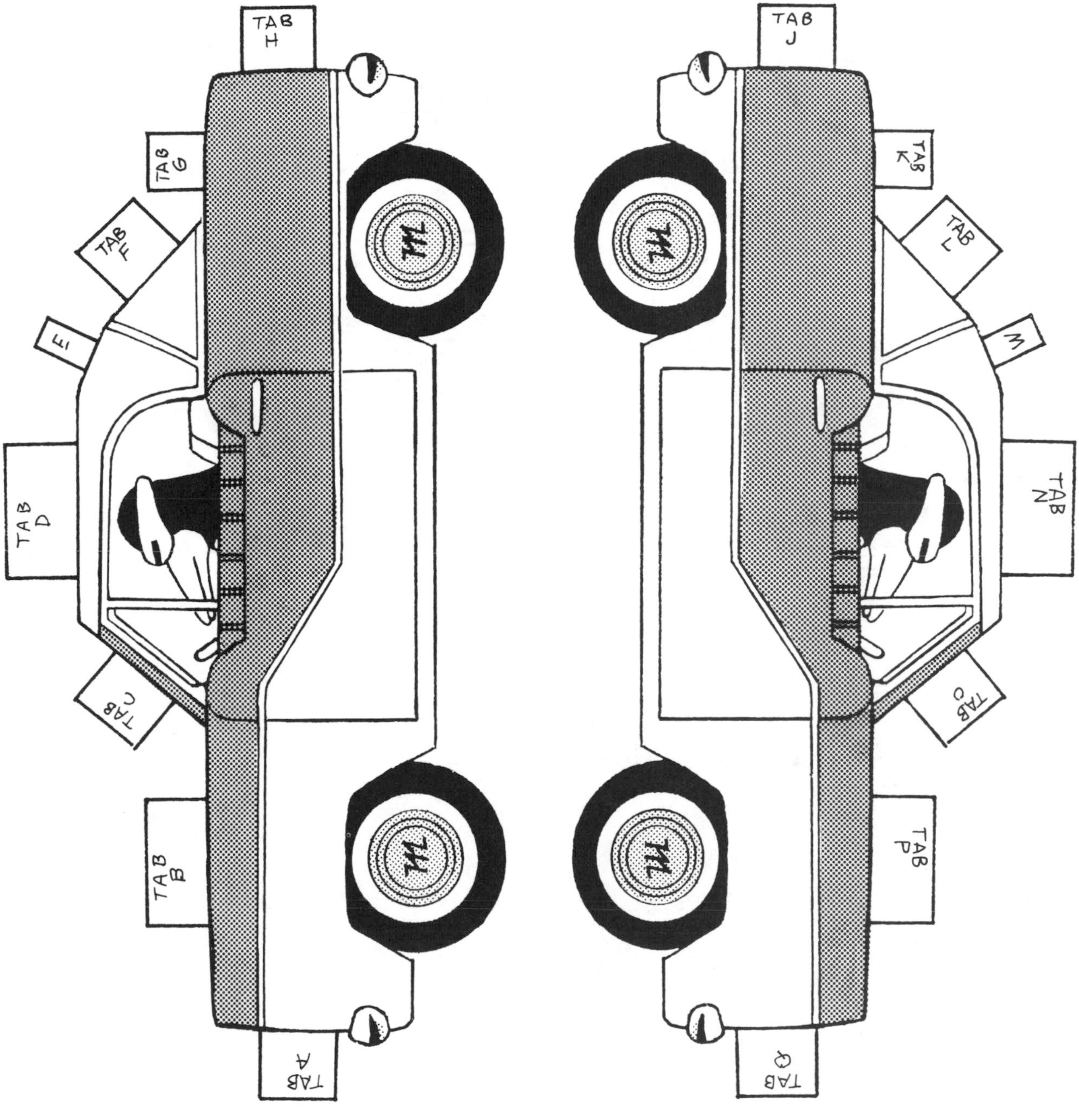

TAB H
TAB G
TAB F
E
TAB D
TAB C
TAB B
TAB A
TAB J
TAB K
TAB L
M
TAB N
TAB O
TAB P
TAB Q

THIS MODERN WORLD

by TOM TOMORROW

ACCORDING TO THE MARCH 1955 ISSUE OF *MECHANIX ILLUSTRATED*, YOU WILL SOON AWAKEN EACH MORNING AS "ELECTRONIC IMPULSES FROM A SUPERSONIC ALARM CLOCK COME DIRECTLY INTO YOUR BRAIN..."

GET UP, YOU LAZY SLUG! TIME TO GO TO WORK! LET'S GET A MOVE ON! HUP! HUP!

PROGRESS...IS...WONDERFUL...

IN MAY 1952, *POPULAR SCIENCE* PREDICTED THAT "ELECTRONIC BRAINS WILL DECIDE WHO IS TO MARRY WHOM...THEREFORE, THERE WILL BE MANY MORE HAPPY MARRIAGES!"

I KNOW IT *SEEMS* STRANGE--BUT THE COMPUTER *SAID* WE WERE *SCIENTIFICALLY COMPATIBLE!*

RIGHT, HONEY?

MOO.

IN 1966, *TIME MAGAZINE* FORESAW A FUTURE IN WHICH "...ONLY TEN PERCENT OF THE POPULATION WILL BE WORKING, AND THE REST WILL, IN EFFECT, HAVE TO BE PAID TO BE IDLE..."

HERE'S YOUR GOVERNMENT HANDOUT, CITIZENS! DON'T WORK TOO HARD *NEXT* WEEK! HA, HA!

HA!

THANKS, MISTER NEWT!

TIME ALSO CONFIDENTLY NOTED THAT, WITHIN A FEW DECADES, "BACTERIAL AND VIRAL DISEASES WILL HAVE BEEN VIRTUALLY WIPED OUT. PROBABLY ARTERIOSCLEROTIC HEART DISEASE WILL ALSO HAVE BEEN ELIMINATED."

MAN--THEY GOT *THAT* ONE RIGHT, TOO!

YES, THEIR ACCURACY WAS *UNCANNY!* IT'S NO *WONDER* SOCIETY HOLDS FUTURISTS IN SUCH *HIGH REGARD!*

*TIME QUOTES BY WAY OF THE *NY TIMES* MAGAZINE, 12-24-95.

THIS MODERN WORLD
by TOM TOMORROW

Panel 1:
WHY IS THE AMERICAN PUBLIC SO CRANKY ABOUT THE *ECONOMY* THESE DAYS, ANYWAY? AFTER ALL, A MULTITUDE OF PUNDITS *INSIST* THAT THINGS ARE *GREAT!*

AND WE HAVE *STATISTICS* TO PROVE IT!

NOT TO MENTION *COLORFUL CHARTS!*

Panel 2:
WELL, THIS IS JUST A *CRAZY GUESS* -- BUT *MAYBE* THE PUBLIC HAS BEGUN TO SUSPECT THAT THE *EXPERTS* HAVE A VERY PECULIAR IDEA OF WHAT CONSTITUTES *GOOD ECONOMIC NEWS*...

--AND GIGANTICO STOCK *SOARED* TODAY AFTER 17,000 EMPLOYEES WERE --AH-- *DOWNSIZED!* INVESTORS MADE A *BUNDLE!*

HEY, THAT'S *TERRIFIC!*

GRRR...

NOTICE OF TERMINATION

Panel 3:
OR PERHAPS THIS SENSE OF UNEASE CAN BE TRACED TO THE FACT THAT MANUFACTURING JOBS ARE DISAPPEARING OVERSEAS AT *RECORD* RATES... OR THAT THE NATION'S LARGEST EMPLOYER IS NOW A *TEMP AGENCY*...

GREAT NEWS! THE BOSS SAID I CAN WORK *NEXT* WEEK, TOO!

GEEZ--I WISH *I* HAD THAT MUCH JOB SECURITY!

Panel 4:
THEN AGAIN, PERHAPS THE AMERICAN PUBLIC IS SIMPLY *INSANE*.

YES--THAT'S *IT!* THE ENTIRE COUNTRY IS *DELUSIONAL!*

IT'S THE *ONLY PLAUSIBLE EXPLANATION!*

WE'D BETTER GET TO WORK ON SOME *CHARTS!*

TOM TOMORROW©4-12-95...Tomorrow@well.com

THIS MODERN WORLD

by TOM TOMORROW

IT JUST DOESN'T MAKE ANY SENSE TO ME...YOU REPUBLICANS SEEM TO *FLAUNT* YOUR HYPOCRISY AND INCONSISTENCY! YOU ARGUE THAT HOLLYWOOD MOVIES & RAP MUSIC AFFECT THE MORAL FIBER OF AMERICA, BUT THAT HATE TALK RADIO HAS NO IMPACT WHATSOEVER...

YOU INSIST THAT YOU CAN BALANCE THE BUDGET *AND* GIVE THE WEALTHY A TAX CUT...YOU'VE GONE FROM CLAIMING THAT THERE'S NOTHING WHATSOEVER WRONG WITH OUR HEALTH CARE SYSTEM TO ARGUING THAT MEDICARE IS ABOUT TO BANKRUPT US...I JUST DON'T *GET* IT!

WELL, THE ANSWER IS *SIMPLE*, PENGUIN! YOU SEE, WE REPUBLICANS--

--ARE ACTUALLY *SPACE ALIENS!*..SENT TO THIS PLANET TO DETERMINE JUST HOW *STUPID* AND *GULLIBLE* YOU EARTHLINGS CAN POSSIBLY *BE!* HA HA HA HA HA HA HA HA HA!

AIEEEEEEE!

SPARKY, WILL YOU HOLD IT *DOWN* IN THERE?

ZZZZ--WHA--OH...

WELL, YOU HAVE TO ADMIT--IT *WOULD* EXPLAIN A LOT...

THIS MODERN WORLD
by TOM TOMORROW

Panel 1:
SPARKY, EVEN *YOU* CAN'T ARGUE WITH MISTER NEWT ABOUT THE NEED FOR *TORT REFORM!* I MEAN--HAVE YOU HEARD ABOUT THE *WHINER* WHO SUED McDONALD'S BECAUSE SHE SPILLED HOT COFFEE IN HER LAP--AND WAS AWARDED *THREE MILLION DOLLARS?*

WHY, YES, I HAVE, BIFF...

Panel 2:
THAT "WHINER" WAS 79 YEARS OLD, AND THE COFFEE WAS SO SCALDING HOT THAT SHE RECEIVED THIRD DEGREE BURNS ACROSS HER GROIN, THIGHS AND BUTTOCKS...SHE UNDERWENT SKIN GRAFTS AND SPENT EIGHT DAYS IN THE HOSPITAL, RESULTING IN A MEDICAL BILL OF MORE THAN $10,000...McDONALD'S OFFERED HER $800.

SO SHE WENT TO COURT, WHERE SHE WAS AWARDED THE FAMOUS $3 MILLION SETTLEMENT--

Panel 3:
--WHICH, INCIDENTALLY, SHE NEVER *RECEIVED*, SINCE IT--LIKE ALMOST *ALL* PUNITIVE DAMAGES AWARDED BY JURIES--WAS LATER REDUCED SUBSTANTIALLY.

Panel 4:

Panel 5:
OH.

FACTS REALLY TAKE THE FUN OUT OF ANECDOTAL EVIDENCE, DON'T THEY BIFF?

TOM TOMORROW © 4-5-95

67

THIS MODERN WORLD

by TOM TOMORROW

OVER THE PAST FEW YEARS, AN UGLY SIDE OF AMERICA HAS GROWN INCREASINGLY VOCAL... THINLY-VEILED HATRED AND BILE HAVE COME TO DOMINATE MUCH OF THE NATIONAL DISCOURSE... SELF-STYLED PATRIOTS HAVE WRAPPED THEMSELVES IN THE FLAG WHILE BELITTLING THE VERY VIRTUES OF COMPASSION AND TOLERANCE FOR WHICH THAT FLAG STANDS... AND NOW IT APPEARS THAT A FEW SICK AND TWISTED INDIVIDUALS HAVE TAKEN IT ALL MUCH TOO FAR...

THE FIRST SUSPECT ARRESTED WAS REPORTEDLY A MEMBER OF A "CITIZEN'S MILITIA"... OFTEN LINKED TO WHITE SUPREMACIST ORGANIZATIONS, THESE PARAMILITARY GROUPS HAVE BEGUN TO POP UP IN BACKWOODS SETTINGS ACROSS THE COUNTRY-- STOCKPILING WEAPONS AND EXCHANGING BIZARRE, PARANOID FANTASIES ABOUT ZIONIST CONSPIRACIES AND SECRET WORLD GOVERNMENTS...

IF THIS BOMBING **WAS** THE WORK OF THESE ANGRIEST OF ANGRY WHITE MEN, THEN WE HAVE CROSSED AN AWFUL THRESHOLD... ONLY TIME WILL TELL WHAT THE BOMBERS HOPED TO ACCOMPLISH BY MURDERING SCORES OF INNOCENT AMERICANS IN COLD BLOOD-- INCLUDING AT LEAST 17 SMALL CHILDREN IN A *DAY CARE CENTER*--

--BUT APPARENTLY THE ANSWER TO THAT PLAINTIVE QUESTION ASKED SEVERAL YEARS AGO BY THE MAN WHO UNWITTINGLY SERVED AS THE FLASHPOINT FOR THE L.A. RIOTS-- "CAN'T WE ALL JUST GET ALONG?"--

--REMAINS A RESOUNDING AND TERRIBLE *"NO."*

68

THIS MODERN WORLD by TOM TOMORROW

WHEN THE PRESIDENT INDIRECTLY ACCUSED TALK RADIO OF HELPING TO CREATE THE CLIMATE WHICH SPAWNED THE OKLAHOMA CITY BOMBING, RUSH LIMBAUGH RESPONDED WITH *RIGHTEOUS INDIGNATION*...INSISTING THAT HIS SHOW IS SIMPLY AN INNOCENT DISCUSSION OF THE ROLE OF GOVERNMENT -- "THE SORT OF DEBATE WHICH HAS BEEN GOING ON IN THIS COUNTRY FOR 200 YEARS..."

HOW ABOUT THIS: "ALL MEN ARE CREATED EQUAL--EXCEPT FOR *LIBERAL WACKOS!*"

YES--AND *FEMINAZIS!*

OF COURSE, RUSH ISN'T THE ONLY TALK SHOW HOST OUT THERE...IN COLORADO SPRINGS, FOR INSTANCE, THERE'S A MAN NAMED *CHUCK BAKER*...

--WHO, ACCORDING TO THE MEDIA-WATCH JOURNAL *EXTRA!*, "MIMICS THE SOUND OF A FIRING PIN-- '*KCHING-KCHING*'-- AS HE RAVES AGAINST THE GOVERNMENT AND TALKS TO LISTENERS ABOUT SHOOTING MEMBERS OF CONGRESS & FORMING GUERILLA CELLS..."

AND WE CERTAINLY CAN'T FORGET *G. GORDON LIDDY*, WHO HAS DISCUSSED THE BEST WAY TO KILL A.T.F. AGENTS WEARING BODY ARMOR ("SHOOT FOR THE HEAD")...

--*AND* WHO DESCRIBED HOW TO BUILD A BOMB WHICH "WOULD TAKE OUT A BUILDING"--

--*AFTER* THE TRAGEDY IN OKLAHOMA CITY.

THERE ARE EQUALLY PROVACATIVE HOSTS IN CITIES ACROSS THE COUNTRY...NEXT TO THESE GUYS, RUSH SOUNDS LIKE--WELL--A *TREE-HUGGING LIBERAL*...

HEY, IF THE SPOTTED OWL CAN'T, LIKE, GROOVE WITH THE TIMBER INDUSTRY, MAN--

--THEN IT SHOULD, LIKE, *MELLOW OUT!*

YOU DIG?

THIS MODERN WORLD
by TOM TOMORROW

Panel 1: OKAY...THE WELFARE BUREAUCRACY IS UNDENIABLY DEHUMANIZING AND IN NEED OF REFORM...BUT DOES THAT MEAN THAT WE SHOULD DISMANTLE OUR *ENTIRE SOCIAL SAFETY NET?*

ABSOLUTELY! ENSURING THE BASIC NECESSITIES OF SURVIVAL FOR THE WEAK AND INDIGENT MEMBERS OF OUR SOCIETY--

--IS--LET'S SEE, I KNOW IT'S IN HERE SOMEWHERE--

--AH, YES--"A *LIBERAL PLOT* TO ENCOURAGE *DEPENDENCY!*"

REPUBLICAN CATCHPHRASES FOR EVERY OCCASION

Panel 2: CONSIDER THAT *CORPORATE* WELFARE RUNS AS HIGH AS *$100 BILLION* A *YEAR*...DWARFING SOCIAL SPENDING AND PRESENTING A MUCH MORE OBVIOUS TARGET FOR THE BUDGETARY AX...

WAIT--HERE IT IS--"CORPORATE SUBSIDIES ARE *VITAL* TO ECONOMIC GROWTH!"

AND CORPORATE CONTRIBUTIONS ARE *VITAL* TO YOUR CAMPAIGN COFFERS, EH CONGRESSMAN?

HEH, HEH. WHAT A CUTE LITTLE FELLOW. WHO LET YOU IN HERE?

Panel 3: FRANKLY, *WE* CAN'T HELP BUT WONDER HOW MANY AMERICANS WHO BELIEVE THAT WELFARE SHOULD BE ABOLISHED MAY ONE DAY THEMSELVES NEED A HELPING HAND--CONSIDERING THAT THE GAP BETWEEN THE RICH AND POOR IS WIDER IN THE U.S. THAN IN ANY OTHER WESTERN NATION--

AHEM--"THE AMERICAN PEOPLE ARE *TIRED* OF *CLASS WARFARE!* WHY, THEY--"

OH, GIVE ME THAT.

HEY!

REPUBLICAN CATCHPHRASES FOR EVERY OCCASION

Panel 4: --AND THAT THE FEDERAL RESERVE DELIBERATELY *TRIES* TO MAINTAIN AN UNEMPLOYMENT RATE OF ABOUT *8 MILLION PEOPLE*, TO FORESTALL INFLATION...WHICH, TO PUT THINGS IN PERSPECTIVE, IS MORE PEOPLE THAN LIVE IN NEW MEXICO, ARIZONA, AND IOWA *COMBINED*...

THINK ABOUT *THAT* THE NEXT TIME YOUR FAVORITE WELL-PAID TALK SHOW HOST STARTS RANTING ABOUT ALL THE *BUMS* ON *WELFARE*...

MY BOOK--MUST HAVE MY BOOK--

REPUBLICAN CATCHPHRASES FOR EVERY

TOM TOMORROW ©5-31-95

THIS MODERN WORLD

by TOM TOMORROW

THE PENTAGON RUNS A SCHOOL IN FORT BEN-NING, GEORGIA WHICH HAS TRAINED, AMONG OTHERS, AN ORGANIZER OF SALVADORAN **DEATH SQUADS**, THE HEAD OF AN ARGENTINE **JUNTA**, AND **MANUEL NORIEGA**...

GOOD MORNING, CLASS! TODAY WE'LL BE STUDY-ING **ADVANCED INTERROGATION TECHNIQUES**!

CAN **YOU** SAY "**CATTLE PROD**"?

ANOTHER GRADUATE IS COL. **JULIO ALPIREZ**, THE GUATEMALAN OFFICER ON THE CIA PAYROLL WHO MURDERED AN AMERICAN HOTELIER AND A REBEL LEADER MARRIED TO AN AMERICAN... WHEN COL. ALPIREZ'S EXPLOITS WERE REVEALED BY HOUSE INTELLIGENCE COMMITTEE MEMBER ROBERT TORICELLI, **NEWT GINGRICH** RESPOND-ED **SWIFTLY**...

...DEMANDING THE PUNISH-MENT OF **TORICELLI**.

IT'S AN **OUTRAGE**--

--THAT THIS IN-FORMATION WAS MADE PUBLIC, I MEAN!

NOW THAT THE CAT **IS** OUT OF THE BAG, A PREDICTABLE SCENARIO WILL UNFOLD...HEAR-INGS WILL BE HELD...SHOCK WILL BE PROFESS-ED...AND FINALLY, THE CIA WILL LOUDLY AND PUBLICLY DECLARE THE ENTIRE MATTER A **DREADFUL ABERRATION** WHICH WAS ENTIRELY THE FAULT OF A CONVENIENT, TO-BE-DETER-MINED **SCAPEGOAT**...

UM--YOU SEE-- **ALDRICH AMES** DID IT!

YEAH! THAT'S THE TICKET! THAT **SCOUNDREL**!

THE MEDIA WILL UNDOUBTEDLY COOPERATE EAGERLY WITH THIS RITUAL OF ABSOLU-TION...DOING THEIR BEST TO IGNORE OUR COUNTRY'S ONGOING COMPLICITY IN THE DEATHS OF SOME **110,000 GUATEMALANS** AT THE HANDS OF SUCCESSIVE U.S.-BACKED DICTATORSHIPS OVER THE PAST 30 YEARS...

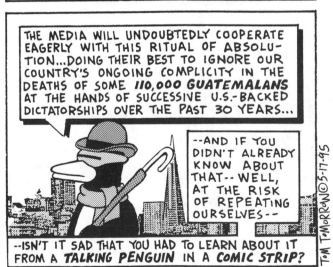

--AND IF YOU DIDN'T ALREADY KNOW ABOUT THAT-- WELL, AT THE RISK OF REPEATING OURSELVES--

--ISN'T IT SAD THAT YOU HAD TO LEARN ABOUT IT FROM A **TALKING PENGUIN** IN A **COMIC STRIP**?

THIS MODERN WORLD
by TOM TOMORROW

Panel 1:

ACCORDING TO A RECENT POLL, TWENTY-FIVE PERCENT OF AMERICANS DOUBT THAT THE HOLOCAUST ACTUALLY *OCCURRED*...

WHY--THIS IS *TERRIBLE!* CLEARLY THE ENTIRE AMERICAN EDUCATIONAL SYSTEM IS AN *ABJECT FAILURE!* SWEEPING REFORMS MUST BE INSTITUTED *IMMEDIATELY!*

Panel 2:

THERE'S JUST ONE PROBLEM--THE QUESTION WAS PHRASED CONFUSINGLY...AND WHEN IT WAS STATED MORE CLEARLY IN A SECOND POLL, THAT FIGURE DROPPED TO *ONE* PERCENT...

OH! HEH, HEH...

NEVER MIND!

Panel 3:

IT SERVES TO DEMONSTRATE HOW EASILY STATISTICS CAN BE MANIPULATED...A FACT TO KEEP IN MIND WHENEVER YOU SEE "EXPERTS" ON MACNEIL-LEHRER OR NIGHTLINE WAVING NUMBERS AROUND...

--AND 97% OF THE AMERICAN PEOPLE BELIEVE THAT THIS COUNTRY'S OFFICIAL LANGUAGE SHOULD BE *PIG LATIN!*

EALLYRAY? ELLWAY, UMBERSNAY ON'TDAY *IELAY!*

Panel 4:

LET'S FACE IT...MOST POLLS AND STATISTICS ARE NOTHING MORE THAN AN ATTEMPT TO GIVE *OPINIONS* AND *IDEOLOGY* A VENEER OF *SCIENTIFIC OBJECTIVITY*...

GOSH--HOW OFTEN WOULD YOU SAY THAT'S THE CASE?

OH, APPROXIMATELY *93.8%* OF THE TIME...

TOM TOMORROW © 8-17-94

THIS MODERN WORLD by TOM TOMORROW

A FEW YEARS AGO, A FOCUS GROUP WAS CONVENED IN SAN FRANCISCO AND SHOWN PRELIMINARY SKETCHES OF ADS TOUTING SOCIAL SECURITY'S OVERALL *STABILITY* AND *TRUSTWORTHINESS*...

SOCIAL SECURITY

THERE'S ABSOLUTELY NO REASON TO BE CONCERNED! HONEST!

WELL--DOES *THIS* ONE RE-ASSURE YOU?

THAT ANYONE WAS EVEN *CONSIDERING* SUCH A CAMPAIGN SAYS MUCH ABOUT THE LEVEL OF PUBLIC CONFIDENCE IN THE SYSTEM....AS DOES THE CURRENT GLUT OF YOUNG WOULD-BE PUNDITS HOPING TO USE THE ISSUE AS A *CAREER SPRINGBOARD*...

--AND SO, LARRY, I'VE OUTLINED *MY* PROVOCATIVE SOLUTION TO THIS CRISIS IN MY NEW BOOK, "*GET A JOB, GRAMPS*"--

--AVAILABLE AT FINE BOOKSTORES EVERYWHERE!

IT HASN'T ALWAYS BEEN THIS WAY...PEOPLE USED TO THINK OF SOCIAL SECURITY AS A GIANT *SAVINGS BANK*, WHERE THE MONEY WITHHELD FROM THEIR PAYCHECKS WAS BEING CAREFULLY GUARDED BY *SCRUPULOUS ADMINISTRATORS*...

ANOTHER DEPOSIT FOR THE ACCOUNT OF TOM TOMORROW, SIR!

AH YES, THAT CAR-TOONIST FELLOW! HERE, LET'S TAKE CARE OF THAT *PROMPTLY*!

NOW, OF COURSE, THE SYSTEM IS POPULARLY BELIEVED TO BE ON THE VERGE OF *BANK-RUPTCY*... AND MANY YOUNG AMERICANS SUSPECT THAT THEY ARE JUST AS LIKELY TO WIN THE *LOTTERY* AS TO EVER RECEIVE SOCIAL SECURITY BENEFITS THEMSELVES...

WHY, THAT'S NOT TRUE AT *ALL*!

WE HAVE A *MUCH* BETTER CHANCE OF WINNING THE LOTTERY!

THIS MODERN WORLD
by TOM TOMORROW

POLITICAL PARTIES OFTEN COORDINATE A PRE-DETERMINED 'LINE OF THE DAY'... FAXING OUT 'TALKING POINTS' TO BE REITERATED DURING NEWS INTERVIEWS & PUBLIC APPEARANCES...

RUSH LIMBAUGH HAS BEEN EXPLAINING THIS FACT OF POLITICAL LIFE TO HIS TV VIEWERS LATELY--BY SHOWING CLIPS OF VARIOUS DEMOCRATS WHO ARE OBVIOUSLY READING FROM THE SAME SCRIPT...

WE DO NOT KNOW IF HIS AUDIENCE'S APPRECIATIVE SNICKERS ARE A MEASURE OF THEIR *IGNORANCE* OR THEIR *HYPOCRISY*, GIVEN THAT THE *REPUBLICANS* HAVE ELEVATED THE USE OF TALKING POINTS TO AN *ART FORM* SINCE LAST NOVEMBER...

IN FACT, AS FAR AS *WE* CAN TELL, THE ABILITY TO MINDLESSLY RECITE THE PARTY LINE IS THE ONLY SKILL *REQUIRED* OF REPUBLICAN REPRESENTATIVES THESE DAYS...

74

THIS MODERN WORLD by TOM TOMORROW

SO BIFF...REPUBLICANS WANT TO CONSTITUTIONALLY *MANDATE* SCHOOL PRAYER...

...PUT THE CHILDREN OF WELFARE MOTHERS INTO GOVERNMENT-RUN *ORPHANAGES...**

*ACTUAL PROPOSAL, ASTONISHINGLY ENOUGH.

...AND EVENTUALLY OVERTURN ROE V. WADE--MAKING REPRODUCTIVE CHOICE A CRIME AGAINST THE *STATE*!

SO REMIND ME--WHY WAS IT THAT YOU VOTED FOR THESE PEOPLE?

WHY--TO GET *BIG GOVERNMENT* OFF OUR *BACKS*, OF COURSE!

OF COURSE... HOW COULD I *FORGET*...

TOM TOMORROW©12-7-94

75

THIS MODERN WORLD

by TOM TOMORROW

THIS MODERN WORLD

by TOM TOMORROW

THIS WEEK: A BEHIND-THE-SCENES EXPOSÉ OF *THIS MODERN WORLD!*--THE CARTOON IS PRODUCED AS QUICKLY AND CHEAPLY AS POSSIBLE BY A TEAM OF VITRIOLIC HACKS WITH ABSOLUTELY *NO REGARD* FOR FACTUAL ACCURACY...TURNOVER IS *HIGH*...

SIR--ARE YOU *CERTAIN* THAT NEWT GINGRICH HAS HAD SEX WITH *FARM ANIMALS*?

YOU MUST BE NEW, KID, SO GET THIS STRAIGHT--THE ONLY THING WE CARE ABOUT HERE IS *MOVING PRODUCT!* OK?

THE DISTRIBUTION PROCESS TAKES PLACE IN A POORLY-VENTILATED SWEATSHOP STAFFED BY ILLEGAL IMMIGRANTS, WHO SPEND TWELVE HOURS A DAY STUFFING ENVELOPES UNDER HARSH AND UNFORGIVING SUPERVISION...

DAMMIT--THIS ADDRESS LABEL IS *CROOKED!* GET OUT OF HERE NOW--AND DON'T COME *BACK!*

SPARKY THE PENGUIN--WHO IN REALITY HAS NO INTEREST IN POLITICS WHATSOEVER--OFTEN SHOWS UP FOR WORK COMPLETELY BLASTED AND UNABLE TO REMEMBER HIS LINES...

YOU KNOW, SPEAKER GRINGINCH--UH--GRINSHGIN-- UM-- I MEAN--

OH, WHO GIVES A RAT'S ASS ABOUT CONGRESS *ANYWAY?*

CUT!!

AND THEN THERE'S TOM TOMORROW HIMSELF...A CYNICAL OPPORTUNIST INTENT UPON MILKING THE "LIBERAL CARTOONIST" NICHE *DRY*--UNTIL A BETTER OFFER COMES ALONG, THAT IS...

HOW MUCH? *REALLY?* SURE, RALPH, SEND ME SOME MATERIAL--

--I'D BE *HAPPY* TO SUPPORT THE CHRISTIAN COALITION!

THIS MODERN WORLD

by TOM TOMORROW

HAPPY VALENTINE'S DAY, EVERYONE! AND IF YOU'RE SINGLE, WELL, DON'T DESPAIR! THERE ARE ALL KINDS OF WAYS TO MEET PEOPLE! FOR INSTANCE, MAYBE YOUR **FRIENDS** KNOW SOMEONE WHO'S JUST **PERFECT** FOR YOU...

SO, TELL ME ABOUT YOURSELF!

GOSH-- WHAT'S TO TELL?

OR WHY NOT PERUSE THE **PERSONALS**? AFTER ALL, YOU CAN **ALWAYS** BELIEVE WHAT YOU READ IN **ADVERTISEMENTS**...

UM-- YOU'RE THE "S.W.M. WITH GOD-LIKE PHYSIQUE"?

YOU GOT A PROBLEM WITH THAT?

THE IMPORTANT THING IS TO **KEEP TRYING!** AFTER ALL, YOU'RE AT **LEAST** AS LIKELY TO FIND TRUE LOVE AND HAPPINESS AS TO, SAY, GET HIT BY LIGHTNING WHILE ICE SKATING IN THE NUDE AT ROCKEFELLER CENTER...

KRAAK!

KER-POW!

AND IN THE MEANTIME-- WELL, JUST BE GRATEFUL FOR ALL THE **TIME** YOU'VE GOT TO DO ALL THE THINGS YOU'VE ALWAYS **WANTED** TO DO...

I'VE BECOME QUITE ADEPT AT CONSTRUCTING SCALE MODELS OF THE WORLD'S BRIDGES OUT OF **TOOTHPICKS**!

I'VE DEVELOPED A VERY MEANINGFUL RELATIONSHIP WITH MY GOLDFISH, **FRED**!

ISN'T HE **ADORABLE**?

TOM ("THEY CALL ME DOCTOR LOVE") TOMORROW ©2-14-96

78

THIS MODERN WORLD

by TOM TOMORROW

BENEATH THE HATE SPEECH AND THE GOOFY CONSPIRACY THEORIES, THE MESSAGE OF THE RIGHT-WING MILITIAS IS ESSENTIALLY THIS: *THE GOVERNMENT OFTEN ABUSES ITS AUTHORITY...* THE HELL OF IT IS, WE CAN'T *ARGUE* WITH THAT...

AFTER ALL, IN THIS CENTURY, OUR GOVERNMENT IMPRISONED & SEIZED THE ASSETS OF THOUSANDS OF AMERICANS OF JAPANESE ANCESTRY...EXPOSED SCORES OF UNSUSPECTING CITIZENS TO RADIOACTIVE FALLOUT...

TEST SITE

...AND SPIED UPON AMERICANS WHOSE ONLY CRIME WAS TO DISAGREE WITH THEIR COUNTRY'S FOREIGN POLICY OBJECTIVES, FROM VIETNAM TO EL SALVADOR AND NICARAGUA...THOUGH AS FAR AS THE *MILITIAS* ARE CONCERNED, THESE CONSTITUTIONAL INFRINGEMENTS *PALE* NEXT TO THE OPPRESSION *THEY* FACE...

A FIVE-DAY WAITING PERIOD TO BUY A HANDGUN? FORMS TO BE FILLED OUT?

WHAT *IS* THIS-- *NAZI GERMANY*?!

GUN

OF COURSE, DISTRUST OF THE GOVERNMENT IS NOT EXACTLY CONFINED TO EITHER GUN-TOTING "PATRIOTS" *OR* CRANKY LIBERAL CARTOONISTS...WHICH IS WHY NUMEROUS REPUBLICAN POLITICIANS WILL SPEND THE NEXT YEAR AND A HALF PRETENDING TO DESPISE THE SYSTEM TO WHICH THEY HAVE DEVOTED THEIR *LIVES*...

IF ELECTED, I WILL SHUT DOWN THE *ENTIRE* GOVERNMENT!

I'LL ORDER THE ARMY TO *RAZE* WASHINGTON TO THE *GROUND*!

I INTEND TO DROP A *NUCLEAR BOMB* AND BE *DONE* WITH IT!

PETE '96

PHIL '96

BOB '96

...AND WHICH IS WHY A *THIRD-PARTY* CANDIDACY SEEMS LIKELY IN '96...WHY, MAYBE THAT FUNNY-LOOKING SHORT GUY WHO MADE SUCH A FUSS ABOUT NAFTA WILL DECIDE TO RUN AGAIN...

LOOK--I'M STILL WEIGHING MY OPTIONS.

LOOK WHAT I CAN DO WITH A CHAINSAW, BEAVIS!

HUH HUH! COOL!

WHAT--DID YOU THINK WE MEANT SOME *OTHER* FUNNY-LOOKING SHORT GUY?

TOM TOMORROW © 7-5-95

79

THIS MODERN WORLD

by TOM TOMORROW

DISNEY'S RECENTLY ANNOUNCED INTENTION TO PURCHASE ABC HAS BY NOW UNDOUBTEDLY INSPIRED INNUMERABLE VARIATIONS ON THE SAME CARTOON...*

> COMING UP NEXT-- AN EXCLUSIVE LOOK AT THE EXCITING NEW LINE OF *POCAHONTAS ACTION FIGURES!*

> HERE'S LOVABLE *BRIT HUME* WITH OUR REPORT!

ABC NEWS

*INCLUDING THIS ONE, OF COURSE.

...BUT PAST THE EASY JOKES, THIS MERGER RAISES TROUBLING ISSUES... FOR INSTANCE, HOW WELL WILL THE PUBLIC INTEREST BE SERVED WHEN MOST SOURCES OF INFORMATION ARE CONTROLLED BY A HANDFUL OF CORPORATE CONGLOMERATES?

> IT SAYS HERE THAT DISNEY *REALLY DESERVES* A *LARGE TAX BREAK!*

> THAT WAS ON THE RADIO, TOO!

> AND ON TV! IT *MUST* BE TRUE!

CONSIDER THAT *NBC* IS ALREADY OWNED BY *GENERAL ELECTRIC*-- AND THAT *WESTINGHOUSE* PLANS TO BUY *CBS*...WHICH MEANS THAT TWO OF THE THREE MAJOR NETWORKS WILL NOW BE OWNED BY CORPORATIONS WHICH ARE HEAVILY INVOLVED IN *NUCLEAR POWER* AND *DEFENSE CONTRACTING*...

> THAT COULDN'T *POSSIBLY* AFFECT THE INTEGRITY OF THEIR NEWS DIVISIONS!

> HEAVENS NO! I'M SURE THERE WILL BE *MANY* HARD-HITTING EXPOSÉS OF PENTAGON OVERSPENDING AND THE HAZARDS OF NUCLEAR WASTE!

IT IS ALSO WORTH CONSIDERING THE PROBABLE *REASON* FOR THIS MERGER-MANIA -- CORPORATE AMERICA'S DESIRE TO EXPLOIT THE POORLY UNDERSTOOD, LARGELY HYPOTHETICAL-- BUT UNDENIABLY FORTHCOMING-- *INFORMATION HIGHWAY*...OR INFORMATION *SHOPPING MALL*, AS THE CASE MAY BE...

> GOSH, BIFF-- THERE ARE JUST SO MANY *CHOICES!*

> YES--I CAN'T DECIDE IF I'D RATHER VISIT THE *CHEVRON WEB SITE* -- OR DOWNLOAD THE LATEST *PEPSI INFOMERCIAL!*

TOM TOMORROW©8-16-95

THIS MODERN WORLD

by TOM TOMORROW

WE RECENTLY RETURNED HOME FROM A SHORT TRIP (DURING WHICH WE PAID LITTLE ATTENTION TO THE NEWS), TO FIND THAT BOB DOLE HAS PINNED THE BLAME FOR *ALL OF AMERICA'S PROBLEMS*--

--ON FICTIONAL REPRESENTATIONS *OF* THOSE PROBLEMS?

AND PEOPLE HAVE BEEN SPENDING TIME *DISCUSSING* THIS?

HONESTLY--WE CAN'T LEAVE YOU KIDS ALONE FOR A *MOMENT*!

HATCH SHOW PRINT

...TWAANG

NOT THAT WE'RE NOT *GRATEFUL*... AFTER ALL, SENATOR DOLE HAS MADE IT *EMBARRASSINGLY* EASY FOR US TO GET BACK TO WORK...

ASSAULT WEAPONS DON'T KILL PEOPLE--

--PEOPLE WHO WATCH *QUENTIN TARANTINO* MOVIES KILL PEOPLE!

...PARTICULARLY GIVEN HIS DESCRIPTION OF *TRUE LIES* (A MOVIE FEATURING GRATUITOUS VIOLENCE, ETHNIC STEREOTYPES, AND A DISTURBINGLY MISOGYNISTIC SUBPLOT--NOT TO MENTION A *REPUBLICAN STAR*) AS "FAMILY FRIENDLY"...*

EAT *THESE* FAMILY VALUES--

--YOU GIRLY-MAN *LIBERALS*!

BAM

BAM BAM

*AN ASSESSMENT THE SENATOR QUICKLY AND CLUMSILY RECANTED...

FRANKLY, IT JUST REINFORCES *OUR* PREVIOUSLY-STATED BELIEF THAT REPUBLICANS ARE ACTUALLY *SPACE ALIENS*--SENT TO DETERMINE HOW STUPID WE AMERICANS CAN POSSIBLY *BE*...

OUR TESTS ARE PROCEEDING ACCORDING TO PLAN! *NEXT* WEEK I WILL ANNOUNCE THAT *HOMELESS PEOPLE* ARE RESPONSIBLE FOR *GLOBAL WARMING*!

VERY GOOD! AND *I* WILL INTRODUCE THE *BLINDNESS PREVENTION ACT*--OUTLAWING *MASTURBATION*!

TOM TOMORROW © 6-21-95

THIS MODERN WORLD

by TOM TOMORROW

HEY, LONELY BACHELORS! IT'S TIME FOR ANOTHER LESSON IN THE *ART* OF *LOVE*--WITH YOUR INSTRUCTOR, *MONSIEUR NEWT!*

AH, BONJOUR! LET US BEGIN! ZEE FIRST THEENG YOU MUST DO IS INVITE A YOUNG *CAMPAIGN WORKER* TO YOUR HOTEL ROOM--TO DISCUSS ZEE *MORAL DECAY* OF ZEE *NATION!*

IF YOU DO NOT HAVE A HOTEL ROOM, ZEE FRONT SEAT OF YOUR *CAR* WILL SUFFICE!

NOW, AT THEES TIME, YOU MUST REMEMBER WHAT MONSIEUR NEWT HAS TAUGHT YOU: A WOMAN IS LIKE ZEE *MINORITY PARTY IN CONGRESS*--YOU MUST *BEND HER* TO YOUR *WILL!*

ALORS! NOW YOU ARE READY TO PRACTICE ZEE FINE ART OF *L'AMOUR REPUBLICAIN*--JUST LIKE *MONSIEUR NEWT!*

THEES TECHNIQUE EES *MOST SIMPLE!* YOU ALLOW THE WOMAN TO, HOW YOU SAY, GIVE YOU *ORAL PLEASURE*--ET *VOILA!* IT IS *DONE!* VOUS ÊTES *FINIS!* YOU ARE GIVING HER... *NOTHING! RIEN! PAS DU TOUT!*

THEES WAY, YOU SEE, YOU CAN SAY YOU *HAVE NOT SLEPT WEETH HER!*

OF COURSE, THEES MAY LEAVE *LA JEUNE FEMME* FEELING--EH--*UNSATISFIED*... SO EVEN THOUGH YOU ARE WANTING NOW TO FALL *ASLEEP*, YOU MUST REMEMBER TO WHISPER *SWEET NOTHINGS* IN HER *EAR*--SUCH AS--LET ME *THINK*--

AH, YES, I KNOW-- "DARLING, EEF YOU TELL ANYONE ABOUT THEES-- I WILL SAY YOU ARE *LYING!*"

JOIN US AGAIN NEXT TIME TO LEARN MORE ABOUT *LES MYSTÈRES DES FEMMES*--FROM THE WORLDLY AND SUAVE *MONSIEUR NEWT!*

TOM TOMORROW ©8-23-95... FOR MORE ABOUT NEWT'S *HISTOIRE L'AMOUR,* CHECK OUT THE SEPT. *VANITY FAIR...*

THIS MODERN WORLD

by TOM TOMORROW

THE INTERNET HAS A LANGUAGE ALL ITS OWN, SPARKY...AND *IMHO*,[1] IT MAKES COMMUNICATION MUCH MORE EFFICIENT THAN *IRL*[2]!

BTW,[3] I KNOW YOU'RE KIND OF A LUD-DITE--BUT *FWIW*,[4] IF THERE'S ANY-THING YOU WANT TO KNOW, I PROM-ISE NOT TO *LOL*[5]--EVEN IF YOU'RE JUST REPEATING *FAQ's*[6]! WHY, I WON'T EVEN TELL YOU TO *RTFM*[7]!

<chuckle>

WHAT ARE YOU DOING?

WHY, MAKING A *SIDEWAYS* SMILEY FACE, OF COURSE!

YOU'RE SPENDING TOO MUCH TIME ONLINE, BIFF.

ALL NETSPEAK GUARANTEED GENUINE:[1] IN MY HUMBLE OPINION;[2] IN REAL LIFE;[3] BY THE WAY;[4] FOR WHAT IT'S WORTH;[5] LAUGH OUT LOUD;[6] FREQUENTLY ASKED QUESTIONS;[7] READ THE F-----G MANUAL...

TOM TOMORROW © 7-6-94 ... e-mail: tomorrow@well.com

THIS MODERN WORLD by TOM TOMORROW

FUTURISM IS A GROWTH INDUSTRY THESE DAYS! MORNING NEWS SHOWS JUST AREN'T **COMPLETE** WITHOUT A SELF-PROCLAIMED **CYBERPUNDIT** CHEERFULLY DESCRIBING THE **BRAVE NEW WORLD** AWAITING US **ALL!**

--AND SOON EVERYONE WILL HAVE COMPUTERS SURGICALLY IMPLANTED IN THEIR **NOSES!**

WELL I'LL BE! ISN'T THAT SOMETHING!

OF COURSE, THE FUTURE DOESN'T ALWAYS LIVE UP TO ITS **BILLING**... FOR INSTANCE, YOU MAY HAVE NOTICED A DISTINCT SHORTAGE OF **DOMED CITIES**, **FLYING CARS**, AND **MOON COLONIES** AS WE APPROACH THE MILLENIUM...

GOSH BIFF-- ISN'T LIFE **WONDERFUL** HERE IN THE YEAR 1995?!

YES-- EVERYTHING TURNED OUT **JUST LIKE THEY PREDICTED!**

AND FRANKLY, WE DON'T SHARE THE POPULAR FAITH IN **TECHNOLOGY** AS A **CURE-ALL**... AFTER ALL, OUR **PRESENT-DAY** TECHNOLOGICAL CAPABILITIES ARE ASTONISHING -- AND YET, MUCH OF THE PLANET IS STILL WRACKED BY FAMINE, POVERTY AND WAR...

YEAH-- BUT THERE'S SURE A LOT OF COOL **STUFF** TO **BUY!**

WIRED
WE'RE SO HIP WE COULD JUST PEE

STILL, THE FUTURISTS THRIVE...SERVING AS PROPAGANDISTS FOR A SANITIZED UTOPIAN VISION WHICH--LIKE MANY BEFORE IT-- FAILS TO TAKE INTO ACCOUNT THE MESSY REALITY OF **HUMAN NATURE**...

LAPTOP COMPUTERS WILL LEAD THE WAY TO GLORIOUS NEW VISTAS, COMRADES!

WE MUST SHINE THE LIGHT OF CHAIRMAN GATES' BENEFICENCE UPON ANTI-REVOLUTIONARY LUDDITES EVERYWHERE!

TOM TOMORROW © 9-13-95

THIS MODERN WORLD

by TOM TOMORROW

HEY, BIFF--HOW LONG HAS IT BEEN SINCE YOU CHECKED YOUR *VOICEMAIL*? SOMEONE *MIGHT* HAVE CALLED WHILE YOU WERE OUT!

OMIGOSH-- YOU'RE *RIGHT*!

YOU HAVE *NO* NEW MESSAGES.

LOSER.

NOTHING, EH? WELL, WHAT ABOUT YOUR *E-MAIL*? THERE *COULD* BE AN IMPORTANT NOTE FROM A FRIEND!

To: BIFF@AOBLAH.Com
Subject: Newest O.J. Jokes!

WELL, MAYBE NOT *THAT* IMPORTANT--

--BUT WHAT ABOUT YOUR ANSWERING MACHINE AT *HOME*? HMMM? AND WHAT ABOUT YOUR *PAGER*? MAYBE IT WENT OFF AND YOU DIDN'T HEAR IT! EVER THINK ABOUT *THAT*? AND WHEN WAS THE LAST TIME YOU CHECKED THE *FAX MACHINE*? MAYBE IT RAN OUT OF PAPER IN THE MIDDLE OF AN *IMPORTANT TRANSMISSION*!

MESSAGE RETRIEVAL DISORDER--THE NEUROSIS OF THE NINETIES.

HEY BIFF--GOT A MOMENT TO *TALK*?

NO!! I'M *BUSY!!*

MESSAGES...MUST KEEP CHECKING MY *MESSAGES*...

THIS MODERN WORLD
by TOM TOMORROW

Panel 1:

THE ORIGINAL INTENT OF THE SMITHSONIAN'S ENOLA GAY EXHIBIT WAS TO EXAMINE THE MORAL AMBIGUITY INHERENT IN HAVING DROPPED THE WORLD'S FIRST ATOMIC BOMB...OF COURSE, THIS TURNED OUT NOT TO BE A POPULAR NOTION AMONG ARBITERS OF RIGHT-WING CORRECTNESS...

THOSE POINTY-HEADED INTELLECTUALS WANT TO *REWRITE HISTORY!*

WHY CAN'T THEY JUST BELIEVE WHAT THEY'RE *TOLD*-- LIKE *GOOD AMERICANS!*

Panel 2:

SO RATHER THAN A DISCUSSION OF THE DEVASTATION WROUGHT BY THE BOMB--OR OF THE SUBSEQUENT HALF-CENTURY OF COLD WAR ARMS PROLIFERATION--THE SMITHSONIAN HAS CHOSEN TO PRESENT A VERY INFORMATIVE DISPLAY ON THE ART OF *OLD PLANE RESTORATION*...

IT CERTAINLY IS *SHINY!*

LOOK--HERE ARE THE *CLEANING IMPLEMENTS* THEY USED!

ENOLA GAY

SPONGE   BRILLO PAD

Panel 3:

A SIMILAR DESIRE TO SUGARCOAT REALITY SEEMS TO BE DRIVING CURRENT ATTEMPTS TO REGULATE THE INTERNET, AS WELL AS TV PROGRAMMING... WITH PROPONENTS CITING THE NEED TO PROTECT UNSUPERVISED 'LATCHKEY KIDS' FROM IMAGES OF SEXUALITY AND VIOLENCE...

--AND WHY WASTE MONEY ON ANYTHING SO FRIVOLOUS AS *DAY CARE* AND *AFTER-SCHOOL PROGRAMS*--

--WHEN IT'S SO MUCH MORE POLITICALLY EXPEDIENT TO SIMPLY *UNDERMINE* THE *FIRST AMENDMENT*...

Panel 4:

NOT THAT WE WOULD PRETEND THERE ARE EASY ANSWERS TO *THAT* DEBATE...WE'RE JUST NOT CONVINCED THAT *PALATABILITY TO CHILDREN* SHOULD DEFINE THE LIMITS OF FREE SPEECH FOR *ADULTS* IN *ANY* MEDIUM...

COMING UP *NEXT*--AN EXCLUSIVE INTERVIEW WITH CONTROVERSIAL GREEN-EGGS-AND-HAM ADVOCATE *SAM-I-AM*...

...BUT FIRST, THIS LOOK AT A *LITTLE ENGINE* WHO *THINKS HE CAN!*

TOM TOMORROW © 8-2-95

THIS MODERN WORLD

by TOM TOMORROW

THE "TRUTH" CAN BE A PRETTY NEBULOUS CONCEPT...AFTER ALL, MOST OF US CAN BARELY REMEMBER WHAT WE DID THE NIGHT BEFORE LAST...

NONSENSE! **WE** RENTED THE HEARTWARMING BLOCKBUSTER "FORREST GUMP"!

UM...ACTUALLY I BELIEVE WE SPENT THE EVENING POURING CHOCOLATE SYRUP OVER OUR NAKED BODIES WHILE CHANTING BUDDHIST MANTRAS...

IN **POLITICS**, THIS IS FURTHER COMPLICATED BY THE FACT THAT NO ONE **CARES** WHAT THE "TRUTH" IS...YOU WOULD NEVER HEAR SOMEONE ON **CROSSFIRE** SAYING--

--HMMM...I'VE NEVER LOOKED AT THINGS FROM QUITE THAT PERSPECTIVE...

SAY--DO YOU ALL MIND IF WE STOP THE SHOW **EARLY** TODAY? I NEED SOME TIME TO RECONSIDER MY ASSUMPTIONS!

WHAT MATTERS IN POLITICS IS **IDEOLOGY**... WHICH IS WHY THE MORALISTS WHO DECRY BILL CLINTON AS A DOPE-SMOKING WOMANIZER ARE ABLE TO OVERLOOK CREDIBLE ALLEGATIONS THAT NEWT GINGRICH IS--WELL-- A **DOPE-SMOKING WOMANIZER**...

YES-- BUT HE'S **OUR** DOPE-SMOKING WOMANIZER!

THE LORD MOVES IN MYSTERIOUS WAYS, YOU KNOW!

THIS HOLDS TRUE ACROSS THE POLITICAL SPECTRUM...FOR INSTANCE, THIS MAY NOT BE A POPULAR QUESTION TO ASK, BUT DOES IT STRIKE ANYONE ELSE THAT MANY SUPPORTERS OF DEATH ROW CAUSE CÉLÈBRE **MUMIA ABU-JAMAL** SEEM ULTIMATELY LESS INTERESTED IN HIS ACTUAL **GUILT** OR **INNOCENCE** THAN IN HIS **POLITICAL BELIEFS** AND **SYMBOLIC VALUE**?

JUST **ASKING**, FOLKS... JUST **ASKING**...

WHERE DO YOU WANT THIS BAG OF **HATE MAIL**, MR. PENGUIN?

PROPERTY U.S. POSTAL SERVICE

TOM TOMORROW©9-20-95

THIS MODERN WORLD

by TOM TOMORROW

REPUBLICANS ARE WORKING TO LIFT THE OP-PRESSIVE BURDEN OF GOVERNMENTAL REGULA-TION FROM THE COLLECTIVE SHOULDERS OF THE AMERICAN PUBLIC!

AND NOT A MOMENT TOO SOON!

AMEN!

NO LONGER WILL GOOD OLD-FASHIONED AMERICAN INGENUITY AND RESOURCEFULNESS BE STIFLED BY FACELESS BUREAUCRATS AND PENCIL-PUSHERS IN WASHINGTON D.C!

IT'S ABOUT TIME!

AMERICANS HAVE HAD ENOUGH OF THOSE MED-DLESOME BUSYBODIES!

BACTERIA BURGERS

ACTERIA URGERS

AFTER ALL--EVERYONE KNOWS THAT ALL THOSE RULES AND REGULATIONS ARE NOTHING BUT A POWER GRAB BY BIG-GOVERNMENT LIBERALS!

WHY CAN'T THEY MIND THEIR OWN BUSINESS?

YOU SAID IT, BROTHER!

WHY, WE CAN'T THINK OF A SINGLE INSTANCE IN WHICH GOVERNMENTAL OVERSIGHT IS *EVER* WARRANTED... CAN *YOU*?

NOPE-- SURE CAN'T!

ME EITHER!

THE INVISIBLE HAND OF THE MARKETPLACE IS REGULATION ENOUGH FOR *ME*!

THIS MODERN WORLD

by TOM TOMORROW

THIS CARTOON IS OCCASIONALLY ACCUSED OF EX-CESSIVE *NEGATIVITY*... SO HERE THIS WEEK, TO HELP US EXAMINE A FEW OF NEXT YEAR'S LIKELY PRESIDENTIAL CHALLENGERS, IS OUR NEW SPECIAL GUEST COMMENTATOR -- *BLINKY* THE *VERY LOVABLE DOG*!

ARF! ARF!

I'M *BWINKY*-- AND I *WUV* YOU!

WILL YOU BE MY *FWIEND*?

BOB DOLE, OF COURSE, IS THE CURRENT MEDIA-APPOINTED *FRONT RUNNER*, DESPITE CONCERNS ABOUT HIS ADVANCED AGE -- WHICH HE RECENTLY SOUGHT TO DISPEL BY POSING AWKWARDLY ON A *TREADMILL*...SO WHAT'S *YOUR* OPINION OF THE SENATOR, BLINKY?

UM...I THINK HE IS PROB-ABWY A *VERY NICE MAN*! I WOULD LIKE TO BE HIS *FWIEND*!

PETE WILSON RECENTLY MADE NATIONAL NEWS BY SCUTTLING AFFIRMATIVE ACTION AT THE UNIVERSITY OF CALIFORNIA...ARYAN NATION LEADER RICHARD BUTLER NOTED APPROVINGLY THAT WILSON IS "BEGINNING TO WAKE UP" TO WHITE SUPREMACIST VIEWS...DO *YOU* HAVE ANY INSIGHT INTO THIS CONTENTIOUS TOPIC, BLINKY?

WELLL -- I THINK EVERYONE SHOULD TRY TO BE *FWIENDS*! THEN THE WORLD WOULD BE A MUCH *NICER* PLACE!

AND THEN THERE'S *COLIN POWELL*, WHO HAS YET TO DECLARE EITHER PRESIDENTIAL INTENTIONS OR PARTY AFFILIATION -- AND WHO HAS NOTED THAT WHILE HE CURRENTLY HAS NO POLITICAL PHILOSOPHY, HE *HOPES TO DEVELOP ONE SOON* ...WHAT KIND OF PRESIDENT DO *YOU* THINK THE GENERAL WOULD MAKE, BLINKY?

UM...WELL...I THINK HE WOULD BE A VERY *NICE* PRESIDENT!

?

THAT'S ALL FOR *NOW* -- BUT BE SURE TO JOIN US NEXT TIME, WHEN BLINKY ANALYZES THE *BOSNIAN CONFLICT*!

THIS MODERN WORLD

by TOM TOMORROW

OCCASIONALLY, WE END UP WITH A FEW LOOSE ODDS AND ENDS WE HAVEN'T QUITE MANAGED TO WORK INTO A STRIP...SO, THIS WEEK, A LITTLE *HOUSECLEANING*...

A CYNIC MIGHT CONSIDER THIS AN EXCUSE TO HASTILY CONCOCT A CARTOON FROM SOME HALF-THOUGHT-OUT IDEAS BEFORE TAKING THE WEEK OFF!

HA! SUCH A HYPOTHETICAL PERSON WOULD SIMPLY NOT UNDERSTAND HOW WE *WORK OUR FINGERS TO THE BONE* FOR OUR READERS!

FOR INSTANCE, GIVEN THE CURRENT MANIA FOR *AMENDING* THE *CONSTITUTION*, WE'VE BEEN WANTING TO PROPOSE OUR *OWN* AMENDMENT... BARRING FROM PUBLIC SERVICE ANYONE WHO HAS EVER USED THE PRONOUNCIATION "*FEDRUL GUVMINT*"-- EFFECTIVE *IMMEDIATELY*...

OF COURSE, THIS WOULD ELIMINATE MAYBE *HALF* THE CURRENT CONGRESS...

WHAT A *SHAME*...

SPARKY--HAVE YOU SEEN THE *SUNBLOCK*?

SPEAKING OF *REPUBLICANS*...DOESN'T IT SEEM A LITTLE... *ODD*...THAT A POLITICAL PARTY WOULD SEEK TO CURRY FAVOR WITH VOTERS BY CHAMPIONING *POISONED MEAT, DIRTY WATER*, AND THE RIGHT OF SELF-APPOINTED *MESSIAHS* TO STOCKPILE *WEAPONS* AND SEXUALLY ABUSE *YOUNG GIRLS*...?

...UNLESS, AS *WE* HAVE REPEATEDLY THEORIZED, THEY ARE ACTUALLY *SPACE ALIENS* --

--SENT TO TEST THE LIMITS OF *AMERICAN STUPIDITY*...

AGENT X-57 HERE! RESULTS EXCEEDING OUR WILDEST PROJECTIONS!

FINALLY, A WORD OF WARNING TO THOSE OF YOU WHO DISPLAY OUR NATION'S *FLAG*... YOU SHOULD BE AWARE THAT THE COLORS *RED*, *WHITE* AND *BLUE* HAVE BEEN *COPYRIGHTED* BY THE *POSTAL SERVICE*...

Color Scheme © UNITED STATES POSTAL SERVICE

U.S. MAIL

...AT LEAST, ACCORDING TO A NOTICE ON THE VAN THAT BRINGS *OUR* MAIL... (WE ARE *NOT* MAKING THIS UP...)

TOM TOMORROW © 9-6-95

THIS MODERN WORLD — by TOM TOMORROW

Panel 1:
ON MACNEIL-LEHRER RECENTLY, A CITIZEN'S MILITIA MEMBER EXPLAINED THE SORT OF GOVERNMENTAL OPPRESSION WHICH INSPIRED HIM TO TAKE UP ARMS...

"UM...THERE'S COUNTLESS EXAMPLES...UH... SOME OF THESE, UH, ITEMS ARE-- REQUIRING THAT ON OUR HIGHWAYS WE ONLY DRIVE 55 MILES AN HOUR! *I* READ NOTHING IN THE CONSTITUTION THAT SAYS THAT THE FEDERAL GOVERNMENT CAN TELL ME HOW FAST I CAN DRIVE MY AUTOMOBILE!"

YOU POOR BABY!

Panel 2:
OPPRESSION IS APPARENTLY IN THE EYE OF THE *BEHOLDER*...NOT THAT WE WOULD ARGUE THAT THE GOVERNMENT IS ALWAYS *FRIENDLY* AND *BENIGN*...

HELLO! I'M FROM THE *INTERNAL REVENUE SERVICE!*

I'M HERE TO *HELP* YOU!

BWAH HA HA HA HA HA!

Panel 3:
NOR WOULD WE DENY THAT THERE EXISTS A LONG HISTORY OF LAW ENFORCEMENT AGENCIES OVERSTEPPING THEIR AUTHORITY, FROM *COINTELPRO* TO, YES, *WACO*...

--BUT IT *DOES* SEEM UNLIKELY THAT SUCH ABUSES WILL BE ERADICATED BECAUSE A BUNCH OF HEAVILY ARMED GUYS NAMED "BUBBA" SPEND THEIR WEEKENDS RUNNING AROUND THE WOODS IN CAMO FATIGUES...

Panel 4:
...AND AT ANY RATE, IT'S NOT AS IF THESE SELF-APPOINTED "CONSTITUTIONALISTS" HAVE BEEN ESPECIALLY ACTIVE IN, SAY, THE CIVIL RIGHTS MOVEMENT...THE CONSTITUTION THEY DEFEND SEEMS TO BEGIN AND END WITH THE *SECOND AMENDMENT*...

Y'SEE--IF I DON'T STOCKPILE *GUNS*-- THEN THE GUV'MINT WILL TAKE MY *GUNS* AWAY!

BUT THEY CAIN'T *DO* THAT-- LONG AS I GOT PLENTY OF *GUNS!*

Y'SEE?

TOM TOMORROW ©5-24-95

91

THIS MODERN WORLD

by TOM TOMORROW

HEY CORPORATE LEADERS! ARE AMERICAN WORKERS--AND THEIR GREEDY DEMAND FOR A *LIVING WAGE*--CUTTING TOO DEEPLY INTO YOUR *PROFIT MARGINS*? WELL, BEFORE YOU MOVE YOUR FACTORIES *OVERSEAS*, WHY NOT CONSIDER USING GOOD OLD-FASHIONED AMERICAN *PRISON LABOR*?

TWENTY CENTS AN HOUR--AND THEY DON'T CALL IN SICK TO GO TO A BALL GAME!

CHINA'S GOT *NOTHING* ON US!

YES, THAT'S RIGHT! YOU CAN *AFFORD* TO KEEP THAT "MADE IN THE U.S.A." LABEL ON YOUR PRODUCTS--WITH *PRISON LABOR*! AND YOU WON'T BE *ALONE*! INMATES IN THIS COUNTRY HAVE *ALREADY* BEEN PUT TO WORK MAKING JEANS FOR *K-MART*...ROCKING PONIES FOR *EDDIE BAUER*...UNIFORMS FOR *McDONALDS*...THE LIST GOES ON AND ON!

AND THEY'RE SUCH *COMPLIANT* WORKERS!

AND THAT'S NOT ALL! INMATES HAVE *ALSO* BEEN USED AS *TELEMARKETERS*...AS OPERATORS BOOKING ROOMS FOR MAJOR *MOTEL CHAINS*...WHY, THEY EVEN TAKE RESERVATIONS FOR *TRANS WORLD AIRLINES*!

HEH, HEH...YEAH, I GOT YER CREDIT CARD NUMBER, ALL RIGHT...

SO DO YOUSE WANTS *AISLE* OR *WINDOW*?

SO DON'T MISS OUT! AFTER ALL, WITH SALES FROM PRISON INDUSTRIES EXPECTED TO REACH $8.9 *BILLION* BY THE END OF THE DECADE...AND WITH A GREATER PERCENTAGE OF OUR POPULATION INCARCERATED THAN ANY OTHER WESTERN NATION...LETTING A BUSINESS OPPORTUNITY LIKE THIS PASS YOU BY--WELL--WOULD BE A *CRIME*!

THIRD WORLD WAGES RIGHT HERE AT HOME? IT'S A DREAM COME TRUE!

MY FAITH IN THE FREE MARKET HAS CERTAINLY BEEN RESTORED!

SLAVE LABOR INC

NOTE: FACTS CITED ABOVE ARE MOSTLY FROM AN ARTICLE IN THE 9-8-95 MADISON *ISTHMUS*, CURRENTLY ACCESSIBLE (BY PERMISSION OF THE AUTHOR) ON THE T.M.W. WEB PAGE: http://www.well.com/user/tomorrow

THIS MODERN WORLD

by TOM TOMORROW

WE'RE CERTAINLY GLAD THAT, IN THIS POST-COLD-WAR ERA, THE C.I.A. IS STILL ABLE TO FIND VERY IMPORTANT THINGS TO DO... LIKE SPYING ON FRANCE...

COMMENT ALLEZ-VOUS, MIREILLE?

JE VAIS BIEN. ET VOUS?

I CAN'T UNDERSTAND A WORD THEY'RE SAYING.

IT MUST BE SOME SORT OF CODE! WHAT ARE THEY TRYING TO HIDE?

YES, WE MAY BE LIVING IN A TIME OF AUSTERITY... BUT BY GOD, THERE'S ALWAYS ENOUGH MONEY FOR MATTERS OF NATIONAL SECURITY!

YOU JUST CAN'T TRUST THOSE DAMNED BAGUETTE-EATERS!

IF IT WERE UP TO ME, WE'D LAUNCH A PRE-EMPTIVE STRIKE TOMORROW-- JUST TO BE SAFE!

CLOSER TO HOME, SPEAKER GINGRICH HASN'T LET THE NEED TO CUT COSTS AND "DEVOLVE" GOVERNMENT STAND IN THE WAY OF HIS NEED FOR AN INCREASED OFFICE BUDGET AND A LARGER STAFF...

WAAAH! YOU'RE NOT S'POSED TO KNOW THAT!

SNIFF! IT'S THE LIB'RUL MEDIA'S FAULT!

THEY'RE OUT TO GET ME, YOU KNOW!

NOT THAT WE'RE ACCUSING THE SPEAKER OF ANY SORT OF INCONSISTENCY HERE... AFTER ALL, HE'S JUST ADHERING TO THAT AGE-OLD REPUBLICAN CREDO--

WE'RE ALL IN THIS TOGETHER--

--EXCEPT FOR ME!!

TOM TOMORROW © 3-15-95

93

THIS MODERN WORLD

by TOM TOMORROW

GOOD GOD, BIFF--IT'S BAD ENOUGH THAT REPUBLICANS WANT TO EASE RESTRICTIONS ON SEWAGE IN OUR WATER AND BACTERIA IN OUR MEAT--**NOW** THEY WANT TO REPEAL THE BAN ON OZONE-DEPLETING **CFC's!** WHAT COULD THESE PEOPLE BE **THINKING?**

WELL, SPARKY, THEY BELIEVE THE **COST** OF THE BAN MAY NOT BE "**WORTH**" IT"!

THE **COST**, EH? HMMM...WELL, LET'S CONSIDER THIS **LOGICALLY**... IF THE BAN **IS** IMPLEMENTED AND ULTIMATELY PROVES TO HAVE BEEN UNNECESSARY, THE WORST THING THAT WILL HAPPEN IS THAT A FEW CORPORATIONS WILL LOSE SOME **MONEY**...

IF, HOWEVER, THE BAN IS **REPEALED**-- AND THE FEARS OF ALMOST **ALL** REPUTABLE SCIENTISTS PROVE TO BE **CORRECT**-- WELL--

--**EVERY LIVING BEING ON THE PLANET IS GOING TO BE AT RISK FOR SKIN CANCER, CATARACTS, AND IMMUNE SYSTEM DEFICIENCIES!!**

YEAH, THAT'S A **MIGHTY** TOUGH ONE TO FIGURE OUT! WHAT AN ETHICAL DILEMMA INDEED! WHOO BOY, AM **I** EVER STUMPED! YESIR-**REE**--

I OFTEN DON'T KNOW WHY I BOTHER TALKING TO YOU.

TOM TOMORROW© 11-1-95

THIS MODERN WORLD

by TOM TOMORROW

Panel 1:

THE SIMPSON TRIAL IS FINALLY OVER-- AND AMERICANS HAVE BEGUN TO DRAW CONCLUSIONS ABOUT ITS ULTIMATE MEANING...

ONE THING'S FOR SURE-- IT WAS THE *TRIAL OF THE CENTURY*!

‡COUGH‡ --EXCLUDING THAT LITTLE UN-PLEASANTNESS AT *NUREMBERG*, OF COURSE?

WHERE?

Panel 2:

WE'VE LEARNED MUCH ABOUT OUR LEGAL SYS-TEM... SUCH AS THE ASTONISHING EXTREMES TO WHICH THE CONCEPT OF "REASONABLE DOUBT" CAN BE PUSHED BY A MULTI-MILLION DOLLAR DEFENSE TEAM...

LADIES AND GENTLEMEN OF THE JURY-- YOU MUST ADMIT THE *POSSIBILITY* THAT O.J. SIMPSON *COULD* HAVE BEEN *ABDUCTED BY ALIENS*--

--WHILE *ELVIS* COMMITTED THESE MURDERS!

TIP O' THE PEN (GUIN) TO THOM ZAJAC!

Panel 3:

IN HIS CLOSING STATEMENT, JOHNNIE COCHRAN SUMMARIZED THE DEFENSE'S ARGUMENT WITH A RHYMING COUPLET-- "IF IT DOESN'T FIT, YOU MUST ACQUIT" -- WHICH WAS ALMOST CERTAINLY THE RESULT OF *TEST MARKETING* AND *FOCUS GROUP RESEARCH*...

OKAY-- WHAT DO YOU THINK OF *THIS* ONE?

"IF THE GLOVE'S TOO TIGHT THEN THIS CASE *BITES*!"

Panel 4:

AT ANY RATE, THE TRIAL IS NOW *HISTORY*-- WHICH MEANS THAT THE FIRST WAVE OF O.J. *NOSTALGIA* SHOULD SWEEP THE COUNTRY ANY *DAY* NOW...

HEY FOLKS-- REMEMBER THE *BLOODY GLOVE*? THE *BARKING DOG*? THE *RACIST COP*? WELL, NOW YOU CAN *RE-LIVE* THOSE GOLDEN MEMORIES WITH *"THE BEST OF O.J."* -- NOT AVAILABLE IN ANY STORE!

FOR K-TEL PRO-DUCTIONS -- *I'M* STILL JOHNNIE COCHRAN IN A CAP!

THE BEST OF O.J.!

TOM TOMORROW ©10-18-95

95

THIS MODERN WORLD

by TOM TOMORROW

THESE ARE **DANGEROUS TIMES**, CITIZENS! THERE ARE TERRORISTS LURKING **EVERYWHERE!**

HEY, HON-- WHY IS THERE A HALF-TON OF FERTILIZER IN THE BACK YARD?

UH-- I'M JUST DOING A LITTLE GARDEN-ING...

(A DRAMATIZATION)

OUR GOVERNMENT IS **TRYING** TO PROTECT US, THOUGH! FOR INSTANCE, THE **FBI** WOULD LIKE TO TURN THE DEVELOPING **INFORMATION HIGHWAY** INTO A GIGANTIC **SURVEILLANCE SYSTEM** --CAPABLE OF MONITORING ANYONE'S **PHONE CALLS, E-MAIL** OR **CREDIT CARD EXPENDITURES...**

JUST THINK OF US AS A CARING, WATCHFUL RELATIVE --LIKE A **BIG BROTHER!**

ER--MAYBE I SHOULD REPHRASE THAT...

HEH, HEH...

Fede... Bur... of Inve...ati...

BUT HECK-- WHY STOP **THERE?** WHY NOT GIVE LAW ENFORCEMENT OFFICIALS THE POWER TO SEARCH ANYONE'S **HOME**--AT **ANY TIME**-- FOR **NO PARTICULAR REASON?** THEY'D SURE CATCH PLENTY OF CRIMINALS **THEN!**

COME ON **IN**, OFFICER! **WE** DON'T HAVE ANYTHING TO HIDE!

FOR THAT MATTER, WHY DON'T WE STOP HOBBLING THE AUTHORITIES WITH THE NEED TO GATHER **EVIDENCE** AND HOLD **TRIALS**-- AND SIMPLY ALLOW THEM TO IMPRISON **ANYONE THEY WANT!** AFTER ALL, WHAT'S MORE IMPORTANT--A FEW MEASLY **CONSTITUTIONAL RIGHTS**... OR AN **ORDERLY SOCIETY..?**

BUT--WE DIDN'T **DO** ANYTHING!

YEAH, YEAH...THAT'S WHAT THEY **ALL** SAY...

TOM TOMORROW © 11-8-95

THIS MODERN WORLD

by TOM TOMORROW

USING THE HUBBLE TELESCOPE, SCIENTISTS HAVE DISCOVERED THAT THERE ARE APPROXIMATELY *40 BILLION* MORE GALAXIES IN THE UNIVERSE THAN PREVIOUSLY BELIEVED.

IT'S A NUMBER TOO LARGE TO REALLY COMPREHEND, BUT THINK OF IT THIS WAY: IF YOU COULD SOMEHOW TRAVEL TO A NEW GALAXY EVERY *DAY*, IT WOULD STILL TAKE YOU *136 MILLION YEARS* TO SEE THEM ALL...

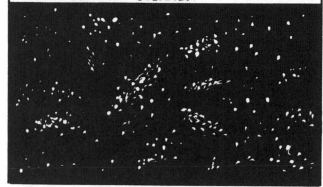

OR, AS THE *NEW YORK TIMES* PUT IT: "UNTIL LAST WEEK THERE WERE ABOUT TWO GALAXIES FOR EVERY PERSON ON EARTH. NOW THERE ARE *TEN* PER PERSON..."

...AND KEEP IN MIND THAT THOSE GALAXIES CONTAIN 50 TO 100 BILLION STARS *EACH*...

KIND OF PUTS THINGS IN PERSPECTIVE, DOESN'T IT?

--A *FLAT TAX!* FITS ON A *POSTCARD!*

--TIME TO *END WELFARE AS WE KNOW IT!*

BLATHER!

BLATHER!

--WE *MUST* BALANCE THE BUDGET WITHIN *SEVEN YEARS!*

BLATHER!

(YAWN...)

(THEY *DO* GO ON, DON'T THEY?)

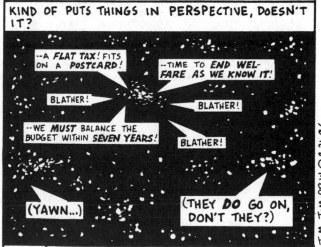

TOM TOMORROW © 2-21-96

THIS MODERN WORLD
by TOM TOMORROW

Panel 1:

THIS IS TRUE: A FRIEND OF OURS RECENTLY HAD A DREAM IN WHICH THE *UNABOMBER* HAD HIS OWN *CHILDREN'S TV SHOW*, COMPLETE WITH A LINE OF *SPINOFF MERCHANDISE*--

HELLO, KIDS! CAN *YOU* SAY "INDUSTRIAL SOCIETY AND ITS FUTURE"? HEH, HEH-- I *KNEW* YOU COULD!

UNABOMBER™ ACTION FIGURE WITH EXPLODING UNMARKED PARCEL!

--ALL WITH THE BLESSING OF THE *FBI*, WHICH CONTINUED TO HOPE THAT INCREASED EXPOSURE MIGHT LEAD TO HIS *CAPTURE*...

Panel 2:

IT ALMOST SEEMS PLAUSIBLE...AFTER ALL, HE BLACKMAILED HIS WAY INTO THE *WASHINGTON POST*-- AND WAS OFFERED A REGULAR COLUMN IN *PENTHOUSE* BY *BOB GUCCIONE*...

Dear Penthouse--I never believed your letters were real until yesterday... I was spending a quiet evening at home preparing a new batch of nitro-glycerin when, to my surprise, my gorgeous neighbor came in, wearing nothing but a flimsy nylon negligee! "Darling," I said, "that's an impure synthetic by-product of the industrial technical system! We must take it off you immediately!"

PENTHOUSE

Panel 3:

FAME IN AMERICA IS A STRANGE THING, AS THE O.J. TRIAL HAS ALSO PROVEN... IT SEEMS THE ONLY PARTICIPANT IN *THAT* CIRCUS WHO DOESN'T HAVE A MOVIE, TALK SHOW, OR BOOK DEAL PENDING IS *KATO* THE *BARKING DOG* -- AND FRANKLY, WE'RE NOT COUNTING *HIM* OUT YET...

ARF ARF ARF ARF ARF!

MAN--THAT DOG TELLS IT LIKE IT IS!

Panel 4:

JUROR BRENDA MORAN PLANS TO HAVE A BOOK OUT WITHIN A MONTH--AND AFTER THAT WHO KNOWS? HOPEFULLY *SOMEONE* WILL COME UP WITH AN APPROPRIATE VEHICLE FOR THE WOMAN WHO SAW NO CONNECTION BETWEEN *DOMESTIC VIOLENCE* AND *MURDER*...

IT'S TIME FOR ANOTHER EPISODE OF *CAUSE AND EFFECT*-- WITH YOUR HOST *BRENDA MORAN*!

OOPS-- I JUST KNOCKED OVER A GLASS OF WATER-- BUT, HEY! HOW DID THIS TABLE GET SO WET?

TOM TOMORROW ©10-25-95 · SPECIAL THANKS TO JONATHAN LETHEM, DREAMIN' MAN...

THIS MODERN WORLD

by TOM TOMORROW

IN CALIFORNIA, THE STATE BOARD OF EQUALIZA-TION HAS DECIDED THAT *CARTOONS* SHOULD BE SUBJECT TO *SALES TAXES*...THE B.O.E. ARGUES THAT SINCE CARTOONISTS USE *PICTURES* AS WELL AS WORDS, THEY DO NOT QUALIFY AS AUTHORS (WHO ARE EXEMPT)--AND THAT THEIR WORK SHOULD BE PLACED IN THE SAME CATEGORY AS *STAPLE GUNS* OR *PLUMBING FIXTURES* OR ANY OTHER *COMMODITY*...

I'LL TAKE A ROLL OF *LIFE SAVERS*, A BOX OF *KLEENEX*-- AND A DOZEN OF THOSE SILLY *SYN-DICATED CARTOONS!*

BY THE B.O.E.'S LOGIC, ART SPIEGELMAN'S PULITZER-WINNING TALE OF THE HOLOCAUST, *MAUS*, WOULD NOT BE CONSIDERED LITERATURE ...NOR WOULD THE WORK OF MAURICE SENDAK, DR. SEUSS, ANTOINE de SAINT-EXUPERY, OR ANY OF A LEGION OF CREATORS WHO HAVE INCOR-PORATED TEXT WITH *VISUAL IMAGERY*...

I CERTAINLY DON'T UNDERSTAND HOW THESE *CARTOONISTS* CAN CONSIDER THEM-SELVES *WRITERS!*

YES--EVERYONE *KNOWS* THAT COMICS ARE NO-THING BUT *FUN-NY PICTURES!*

ACCORDING TO THE BOARD, THE ONLY THING THAT MATTERS ABOUT A CARTOON IS THE MANNER IN WHICH IT IS *DELIVERED* TO *PUBLISHERS* ...IF IT HAS BEEN PRINTED AND *MAILED*, IT IS *TAXABLE*--BUT IF IT HAS BEEN TRANS-MITTED BY *COMPUTER*, IT IS *NOT*...

...SO YOU SEE, TAXES ARE *CLEARLY* DUE ON THE CAR-TOON ON MY *RIGHT*-- BUT NOT THE ONE ON MY *LEFT*...

...OR IS IT THE OTHER WAY AROUND..?

IF THE TAX IS UPHELD, ANY CARTOONIST WHOSE WORK RUNS IN CALIFORNIA (REGARDLESS OF THEIR RESIDENCY) WILL NEED A STATE-ISSUED *SALES PERMIT*...IN OTHER WORDS, FOR THE FIRST TIME IN AMERICAN HISTORY, AN EN-TIRE CLASS OF WRITERS WILL HAVE TO BE *LICENSED* BY THE *GOVERNMENT* IN ORDER TO PRACTICE THEIR CRAFT...

AH, YES, MR. TOMORROW...WE SEEM TO HAVE, ER, *MISPLACED* YOUR APPLICATION...I'M AFRAID YOU'LL HAVE TO *RESUBMIT* IT IN *TRIPLICATE*...

WE SHOULD HAVE AN ANSWER FOR YOU IN *EIGHT* TO *TEN MONTHS*...

CARTOON LICENSES

The cartoonists won.

MORE INFO: http://www.well.com/user/tomorrow

©11-21-95 TOM TOMORROW, THE WORLD'S MOST VERBOSE NON-WRITER

THIS MODERN WORLD by TOM TOMORROW

Panel 1: ACCORDING TO SUCH NOTED CONTEMPORARY PHILOSOPHERS AS NEWT GINGRICH AND RUSH LIMBAUGH, *LIBERALS* WILL SOON BE AS EXTINCT AS *DINOSAURS*...

AND NOT A MOMENT TOO SOON! RUSH SAYS THEY'VE BEEN RUNNING THE COUNTRY FOR *FORTY YEARS*!

THANK GOD THE YOKE OF THEIR OPPRESSIVE *TYRANNY* HAS AT LAST BEEN LIFTED!

Panel 2: LIMBAUGH EVEN FACETIOUSLY SUGGESTS PRESERVING ONE OR TWO OF THESE DANGEROUSLY FOOLISH CREATURES IN SOME SORT OF *MUSEUM* -- AS A CAUTIONARY *REMINDER* FOR FUTURE GENERATIONS...

"LIBERALS"? WEREN'T THEY THE ONES WHO WERE ALWAYS YAMMERING ON ABOUT *TREES* AND *CLEAN AIR*? HA, HA, HA!

HA, HA! SOMETHING LIKE THAT! WHAT A BUNCH OF *WACKOS*!

SAY, WHAT'S A *TREE*?

CARD CARRYING LIBERAL (20th century)

LOVE ME

Panel 3: IRONICALLY, THE TERM "LIBERAL" IS HELD IN *EQUAL* CONTEMPT BY MANY *NATION* READERS... BRINGING TO MIND AS IT DOES FOR *THEM* SOMEONE WHO WAS -- FOR INSTANCE -- *VERY ENTHUSIASTIC* ABOUT THE ELECTION OF BILL CLINTON...

THIS IS *TERRIFIC*, MUFFY! ALL OF AMERICA'S SOCIAL PROBLEMS WILL *CERTAINLY* BE SOLVED *NOW*!

WE CAN FINALLY SCRAPE THOSE UNSIGHTLY *BUMPER STICKERS* OFF THE *VOLVO*!

Daily Whatever — CLINTON WINS

Panel 4: IN FACT, MAYBE IT'S TIME FOR THOSE OF US WHO VAGUELY DESCRIBE OURSELVES AS *PROGRESSIVE* OR *LEFTIST* -- OR SOME DAMN THING -- TO *RECLAIM* THE EPITHET "LIBERAL" FROM *EVERYONE*... MUCH AS GAY ACTIVISTS HAVE PROUDLY CO-OPTED THE WORD "*QUEER*"...

AFTER ALL, THE *DICTIONARY* DEFINES "LIBERAL" AS "GENEROUS... TOLERANT... BROAD-MINDED... IN ACCORD WITH CONCEPTS OF MAXIMUM INDIVIDUAL FREEDOM..."

SEEMS TO ME THERE ARE *WORSE* THINGS TO BE...

©TOM TOMORROW 1995

100

THIS MODERN WORLD by TOM TOMORROW

WITH ASTONISHING CHUTZPAH--NOT TO MENTION A COMPLETE DISREGARD FOR FACTS AS WE ON PLANET EARTH UNDERSTAND THEM--NEWT GINGRICH AND HIS WACKY BAND OF REVOLUTIONARIES HAVE BEEN WORKING TO CONVINCE AMERICANS THAT THE ROOT CAUSE OF *POVERTY* IS ACTUALLY GOVERNMENT AID *TO* THE POOR...

--YOU SEE, THERE SIMPLY *WERE NO POOR PEOPLE* BEFORE THE NEW DEAL!

TRUST ME--I'M SMARTER THAN YOU!

I EVEN WRITE BOOKS!

THEIR ARGUMENTS ARE SO BONEHEADED, THEY ARE DIFFICULT TO PARODY...FOR INSTANCE, DURING A RECENT BROADCAST OF THE *NEWS HOUR* ON PBS, HERITAGE THINK-TANKER ROBERT RECTOR OFFERED THIS ANALYSIS OF OUR NATION'S LONGSTANDING GUARANTEE OF ASSISTANCE FOR NEEDY CHILDREN...

"A.F.D.C. HAS *DESTROYED* THE LIVES OF MILLIONS OF CHILDREN..."

"THIS IS NOT A SAFETY NET--THIS IS A SYSTEM OF *CHILD ABUSE!*" *

...WHILE G.O.P. REPRESENTATIVE CLAY SHAW CHIMED IN WITH *THIS* TRULY PECULIAR PIECE OF REASONING...

"WE HAVE A PROGRAM THAT'S 60 YEARS OLD! (YOU) WOULDN'T CONSIDER A *CAR* THAT'S 60 YEARS OLD TO BE *RELIABLE TRANSPORTATION!*" *

GOSH--WE HAVE A *CONSTITUTION* THAT'S OVER *200* YEARS OLD--SHOULD WE SCRAP *IT*?

DON'T GIVE THEM ANY IDEAS.

*ACTUAL QUOTES, SADLY ENOUGH...

OF COURSE, REPUBLICANS UNDERSTAND THAT THEY MUST AT LEAST *SEEM* TO BE OFFERING ALTERNATIVES--SUCH AS ARIANNA HUFFINGTON'S PLAN TO INSPIRE *INCREASED VOLUNTEERISM* WITH A SERIES OF SLICKLY-PRODUCED *TELEVISION COMMERCIALS*...

AND WHO COULD *POSSIBLY* BE MORE INSPIRING THAN *ARIANNA HUFFINGTON*?

YES--WE CAN ONLY *STRIVE* TO BE WORTHY OF HER *SELFLESS GUIDANCE*...

THIS MODERN WORLD
by Tom Tomorrow

ON A COLD WINTER'S EVENING, *NEWTENEZER GINGRICH* RECEIVES A VISIT FROM A *DREADFUL APPARITION*...

I WEAR THE CHAINS I FORGED IN LIFE... NO SPACE OF REGRET CAN MAKE AMENDS FOR ONE LIFE'S OPPORTUNITY MISSED...

SO YOU WANNA GET TO THE POINT HERE, DICK?

ARIANNA'S COMING BY LATER...

HEED ME, NEWTENEZER...YOU WILL BE HAUNTED BY THREE SPIRITS! WITHOUT THEM, YOU CANNOT HOPE TO SHUN THE PATH I TREAD!

WHATEVER YOU SAY, DICK.

HAVE THEM CALL MY OFFICE, OKAY?

NEWTENEZER LAYS DOWN ON HIS BED AND FALLS ASLEEP UPON THE INSTANT...HE IS AWAKENED LATER BY A NOISE IN HIS BEDCHAMBER...

ARIANNA? IS THAT YOU?

NO, NEWTENEZER... IT IS *I*--

--THE *GHOST* OF *ELECTIONS PAST*!

SOMEHOW YOU'RE NOT QUITE WHAT I EXPECTED.

TO BE CONT'D!

web: http://www.well.com/user/tomorrow ... web: tomorrow@well.com ... Email: tomorrow@well.com TOM TOMORROW©12-6-95

THIS MODERN WORLD
by Tom Tomorrow

(CONT'D) NEWTENEZER GINGRICH IS TAKEN ON A STRANGE JOURNEY BY THE *GHOST OF ELECTIONS PAST*...

WHERE ARE WE?

WELL, NEWTENEZER, THE YEAR IS 1978--AND THAT'S YOU ON THE BED WITH A YOUNG CAMPAIGN WORKER WHO IS DEFINITELY NOT YOUR WIFE...

IF YOU EVER TELL ANYBODY ABOUT THIS--I'LL SAY YOU'RE *LYING!*

*ACTUAL QUOTE, ACCORDING TO ONE OF NEWT'S EX-GIRLFRIENDS...

AND HERE WE ARE IN A HOSPITAL ROOM IN 1980...YOUR WIFE JACKIE IS RECUPERATING FROM CANCER SURGERY--AND YOU'VE STOPPED BY TO LET HER KNOW THAT YOU WANT A *DIVORCE*...

HOW YOU FEELIN'?

UHHHH...

GREAT. THIS WON'T TAKE LONG...

SO, UM, IS THERE SOME POINT TO THIS?

GET WELL

AND *THIS*, OF COURSE, IS THE COURTROOM WHERE JACKIE APPARENTLY HAD TO GO TO FORCE YOU, MR. FAMILY VALUES, TO MAKE YOUR *CHILD SUPPORT PAYMENTS!*

HEY-- I WAS JUST TRYING TO BUILD THEIR *MORAL CHARACTER!* YOU KNOW HOW I FEEL ABOUT *HANDOUTS!*

THERE'S SO MUCH MORE, NEWTENEZER, BUT OUR TIME IS UP... I MUST RETURN YOU FOR YOUR APPOINTMENT WITH THE NEXT SPIRIT...

LUCKY ME. WHY AREN'T YOU GHOSTS HARASSING *BOB DOLE*, ANYWAY?

BECAUSE NEXT TO *YOU*, DOLE LOOKS LIKE THE VERY SOUL OF *WARMTH & CHARITY*...

MORE...

TOM TOMORROW ©12-13-95

THIS MODERN WORLD
by Tom Tomorrow

(CONT'D) NEWTENEZER GINGRICH IS VISITED BY THE SECOND SPIRIT...

NEWT, AS THE GHOST OF ELECTIONS PRESENT, I JUST WANT TO KNOW--WHAT COULD YOU POSSIBLY BE *THINKING* LATELY? FOR INSTANCE, ADMITTING THAT YOU ENGINEERED A GOVERNMENT SHUTDOWN COSTING TAXPAYERS *MILLIONS*-- BECAUSE THE PRESIDENT *SNUBBED* YOU ON AIR FORCE ONE?

AND THIS HABIT OF YOURS OF BLAMING BIZARRE, TRAGIC MURDERS ON DEMOCRATS AND THE WELFARE STATE-- WHAT'S *UP* WITH THAT, NEWT? ARE YOU TRYING TO PUT THE NATION'S POLITICAL SATIRISTS OUT OF BUSINESS-- BY BECOMING A *LIVING SELF-CARICATURE*?

AND, SPEAKING OF *WELFARE*, NEWTIE-- DO YOU *UNDERSTAND* THAT SLASHING THE SOCIAL SAFETY NET--THAT BASIC COMMITMENT FROM A CIVILIZED SOCIETY TO TAKE CARE OF ITS WEAKEST MEMBERS--WILL HAVE REAL CONSEQUENCES FOR REAL PEOPLE WITH NO OTHER OPTIONS?

HEY--I HAVE COMPASSION FOR THE POOR! AFTER ALL--

--I'M THE GUY WHO WANTED TO GIVE THEM A *TAX CREDIT* TO BUY *LAPTOP COMPUTERS!*

YOU'RE *ALL HEART*, NEWT... *ALL HEART*...

SO DO *ALL* YOU GHOSTS HAVE BEAKS AND SUNGLASSES?

MORE...

TOM TOMORROW © 12-20-95 Email: tomorrow@well.com ··· web: http://www.well.com/user/tomorrow

THIS MODERN WORLD
by Tom Tomorrow

(CONT'D) NEWTENEZER GINGRICH WAS VISITED BY THE LAST OF THREE SPIRITS -- THE GHOST OF ELECTIONS YET TO COME-- AND SHOWN A DARK AND DISMAL FUTURE...

HEY--WHAT'S WITH ALL THE POOR PEOPLE? WHY AREN'T THEY WORKING AS INDEPENDENT CONTRACTORS IN THE NEW THIRD WAVE GLOBAL ECONOMY? WHERE ARE THEIR *LAPTOP COMPUTERS*?

HE RETURNED A CHANGED MAN, VOWING TO WORK FOR A BETTER WORLD... AT FIRST, MANY WERE SUSPICIOUS...

OKAY, LISTEN BILL -- IF WE CUT ENOUGH FROM THE DEFENSE BUDGET AND RETURN UPPER-INCOME AND CORPORATE TAX LEVELS TO A PRE-REAGAN LEVEL, I THINK WE CAN BALANCE THE BUDGET WHILE *INCREASING* SOCIAL AND ENVIRONMENTAL SPENDING!

THIS IS A TRICK, RIGHT?

GOD BLESS US EVERY ONE!

...BUT IN TIME, HE BECAME ONE OF THE MOST BELOVED LEADERS OUR COUNTRY WAS EVER TO KNOW...UNDER HIS INSPIRED GUIDANCE, EVEN THE MOST HARD-CORE IDEOLOGUES EVENTUALLY SOFTENED...

YOU KNOW, *DIVERSITY* IS REALLY WHAT MAKES AMERICA GREAT!

AN UNRESTRICTED *IMMIGRATION* POLICY CAN ONLY *STRENGTHEN* US AS A NATION!

AND WHAT PEOPLE DO IN THEIR *BEDROOMS* IS *NOBODY ELSE'S BUSINESS!*

NOTE TO READERS: THE PRECEDING FANTASY HAS BEEN OUR HOLIDAY GIFT TO YOU. WE'LL RETURN NEXT WEEK TO THE *BLEAK REALITY* OF OUR CURRENT POLITICAL LANDSCAPE...WHICH IS, OF COURSE, DOMINATED BY OPPORTUNISTIC HATE-MONGERS, CYNICAL GREEDHEADS, AND HYPOCRITICAL MORALISTS...AND FOR WHICH THERE IS *NO HOPE* OF IMPROVEMENT OR CHANGE...

SO *MERRY CHRISTMAS*, EVERYONE!

WHAT A *HEARTWARMING* CARTOON THIS IS!

INDEED!

TOM TOMORROW ©12-27-95

THIS MODERN WORLD

by TOM TOMORROW

Note: all dialogue taken verbatim from actual Chinese fortune cookies.

Happy New Year, and remember: you will receive good news by mail!

Tip o' the pen(guin) to the Byliners (especially Scott Rosenberg!)

TOM ("SELL YOUR IDEAS, THEY ARE TOTALLY ACCEPTABLE") TOMORROW · 1-3-96

THIS MODERN WORLD

by TOM TOMORROW

IDEOLOGUES ALWAYS NEED **SCAPEGOATS**...WHICH IS WHY WE ARE CURRENTLY FACED WITH THE SAD SPECTACLE OF OVERFED **MILLIONAIRES** BLAMING OUR NATION'S PROBLEMS ON **WELFARE RECIPIENTS**...

OH, NONSENSE! CONGRESS IS TRYING TO **HELP** THE NEEDY--BY TAKING AWAY THEIR **SAFETY NET!**

HMMM... NOT UNLIKE HELPING THE **SICK** BY BLEEDING THEM WITH **LEECHES**...

ACCORDING TO POPULAR WISDOM, THE POOR ARE SIMPLY **LAZY** AND DON'T **WANT** TO WORK... THIS IN A COUNTRY IN WHICH THE FEDERAL RESERVE MANIPULATES INTEREST RATES IN ORDER TO **MAINTAIN** A SURPLUS OF AROUND 8 MILLION UNEMPLOYED WORKERS--TO "FORESTALL INFLATION..."

--WHICH WOULD SEEM TO PLACE THE JOBLESS BETWEEN THE PROVERBIAL **ROCK** AND **HARD PLACE**...

ADDITIONALLY, AMERICAN MANUFACTURING JOBS ARE DISAPPEARING ABROAD IN RECORD NUMBERS... AS OF AUGUST '95, THE DEPT. OF LABOR CERTIFIED THAT **38,148** WORKERS HAVE LOST THEIR JOBS AS A RESULT OF THE **NAFTA** ACCORD...

--IN FACT, THE VAST **MAJORITY** OF CORPORATIONS WHICH PROMISED TO CREATE JOBS UNDER NAFTA HAVE ACTUALLY **LAID OFF** WORKERS--OFTEN DUE TO "SHIFTS IN PRODUCTION TO MEXICO..."

...AS ANY REASONABLY BRIGHT **12-YEAR-OLD** MIGHT HAVE FORESEEN...

FINALLY--TO KEEP THINGS IN PERSPECTIVE-- CONSIDER THAT OUR COST-CONSCIOUS, WELFARE-SLASHING CONGRESS WILL BE SPENDING **$1.4 BILLION** NEXT YEAR ON A SHIP THE NAVY DID NOT ASK FOR--TO BE BUILT, ODDLY ENOUGH, IN THE HOME STATE OF **TRENT LOTT**, CHAIR OF THE SENATE SHIPBUILDING SUBCOMMITTEE...

UM...WELL...AT LEAST HE'LL BE CREATING **JOBS!** HA, HA...HA?

HA, HA...BIFF, YOU GUYS ARE SO FULL OF CRAP, IT'S OOZING OUT OF YOUR **EARS**...

TOM TOMORROW©10-11-95...E-MAIL: Tomorrow@well.com...WEB: http://www.well.com/user/tomorrow

THIS MODERN WORLD

by TOM TOMORROW

SUSPICION THAT HILLARY CLINTON MAY BE GUILTY OF FINANCIAL MISCONDUCT INCREASED RECENTLY WHEN SOUGHT-AFTER WHITEWATER DOCUMENTS APPEARED ON A TABLE IN THE PRESIDENTIAL LIVING QUARTERS--AND NO ONE COULD EXPLAIN WHERE THEY CAME FROM...

> IT'S A COMPLETE MYSTERY TO **US**!

> WE'RE DOING OUR BEST TO LOCATE THE PERPETRATOR!

> PERHAPS **I** CAN BE OF SOME ASSISTANCE!

THE CLINTONS HAVE ALLUDED THAT A **MAID** OR **BUTLER** MIGHT BE RESPONSIBLE*... BUT PERHAPS THERE'S SOME...**OTHER**...EXPLANATION...

> HILLARY CLINTON'S LEGAL DOCUMENTS--TURNING UP IN THE WHITE HOUSE RESIDENCE? HOW COULD THEY HAVE **POSSIBLY** GOTTEN **THERE**, MULDER?

> THEY **CLEARLY** MUST HAVE BEEN PLACED THERE BY **ALIENS**!

> DAMN.

*HONEST TO GOD.

REPUBLICANS ARE DOGGEDLY PURSUING THE TRUTH-- AND WHO COULD BE MORE QUALIFIED TO INVESTIGATE CHARGES OF CORRUPTION THAN MEMBERS OF A POLITICAL PARTY WHICH IS **OPENLY FOR SALE**...

> ··AS WAS MOST RECENTLY MADE CLEAR BY A FUNDRAISING LETTER WHICH READ LIKE A **RESTAURANT MENU**... PROMISING SPECIFIC LEVELS OF ACCESS TO SPECIFIC REPUBLICAN LEADERS IN EXCHANGE FOR SPECIFICALLY LARGE SUMS OF **MONEY**...

> TODAY'S SPECIAL
> HOUSE FRESHMEN

...AND IF YOU THINK A CEO PAYING TENS OF THOUSANDS OF DOLLARS EXPECTS NOTHING MORE THAN A NICE PHOTO FOR HIS OFFICE WALL...WELL, WE'VE GOT A BRIDGE YOU MIGHT BE INTERESTED IN...

> NO, REALLY! I WOULD **NEVER** DREAM OF BRINGING UP SOMETHING SO CRASS AS A **TAX BREAK** AT A TIME LIKE THIS!

> INDEED! TO DO SO WOULD SURELY SPOIL THE MAGIC OF THIS SPECIAL MOMENT!

> ANYBODY GOT A LIGHT?

THIS MODERN WORLD

by TOM TOMORROW

ACCORDING TO RECENT POLLS, SUPPORT FOR THE REPUBLICAN "REVOLUTION" IS WANING AND NEWT GINGRICH IS CURRENTLY ONE OF THE LEAST POPULAR POLITICIANS IN HISTORY--OR SO WE ARE *TOLD*... BUT COULD THESE JUST BE *LIES* FROM THE NEFARIOUS *LIBERAL MEDIA*..?

> GREAT NEWS, COMRADES! OUR DISINFORMATION CAMPAIGN IS BRINGING US EVER CLOSER TO OUR DREAM OF A *SOCIALIST UTOPIA*--

> --AND OUR *ADVERTISING REVENUES* ARE UP *TWENTY PERCENT!*

PRESS

CONSERVATIVES SEEM TO BELIEVE SO...CONTINUING TO BEHAVE AS IF *NOTHING* COULD BE MORE APPEALING TO THE AMERICAN PUBLIC THAN SMALL-MINDED *VICIOUSNESS* AND IDEOLOGICAL *EXTREMISM*...

> I'LL CERTAINLY VOTE FOR ANY POLITICIAN WHO PROMISES TO LET POOR CHILDREN *STARVE SLOWLY TO DEATH!*

> *I* THINK ANYONE WHO MAKES LESS THAN $20,000 A YEAR SHOULD BE *THROWN TO LIONS* ON *LIVE TV!*

CONSIDER, FOR EXAMPLE, CHARGES THAT BOB DOLE IS TOO *LIBERAL*--AND, EVEN MORE BIZARRE, THAT *PAT BUCHANAN* IS ACTUALLY A RAVING *LEFT-WINGER*...

> SURE, HE WANTS TO OUTLAW ABORTION AND BUILD A WALL ALONG THE MEXICAN BORDER--BUT HE SHOWS SOME *MODICUM* OF CONCERN FOR THE FUTURE OF THE AMERICAN WORKER!

> JEEZ-- WHAT A TREE-HUGGING *WACKO!*

OF COURSE, TERMS LIKE "CONSERVATIVE" AND "LIBERAL" DON'T REALLY BEGIN TO DESCRIBE THE NUANCES OF THE POLITICAL LANDSCAPE THESE DAYS...WHEN MOST REPUBLICAN PRESIDENTIAL HOPEFULS SOUND MORE LIKE TEENAGED *ANARCHISTS* THAN MIDDLE-AGED *CAREER POLITICIANS*...

> WHO NEEDS THE GOVERNMENT ANYWAY, MAN?

> YEAH! LIKE, SMASH THE *STATE*, DUDE!

NEWT   Phil   BIAFRA

... web: http://www.well.com/user/tomorrow ... Email: tomorrow@well.com

ToM ToMoRRoW © 1-7-96

109

THIS MODERN WORLD

by TOM TOMORROW

ANOTHER PRESIDENTIAL CAMPAIGN IS UNDERWAY, AND AMERICANS ARE BEING **INNUNDATED** WITH INFORMATION...OF COURSE, MOST OF IT IS **WRONG**...

GOSH--I DIDN'T KNOW THAT BOB DOLE WAS A VETERAN OF THE **CIVIL WAR!**

THAT'S **NOTHING!** I READ THAT BILL CLINTON IS ACTUALLY THE **UNABOMBER!**

AT THE LOWER LEVELS OF THE DEBATE, THERE ARE THOSE WHO RELY ON **RUSH LIMBAUGH** FOR THEIR NEWS AND ANALYSIS...

--AND WHO, ACCORDING TO A NINE MONTH STUDY CONDUCTED BY THE ANNENBERG SCHOOL OF COMMUNICATIONS, CONSIDER THEMSELVES TO BE THE BEST INFORMED OF VOTERS--BUT ARE, IN ACTUAL FACT, THE **LEAST** WELL-INFORMED...

SOMEHOW THIS IS NOT AN EXTRAORDINARY SURPRISE.

A **SLIGHTLY** MORE SOPHISTICATED AUDIENCE RELIES ON THE SHOUTING-PUNDIT SHOWS SUCH AS THE **CAPITAL GANG**--WHOSE PRODUCERS, ACCORDING TO REGULAR PARTICIPANT MARGARET CARLSON, WANT JOURNALISTS--

"--WHO CAN SOUND LEARNED WITHOUT CONFUSING THE MATTER WITH TOO MUCH KNOWLEDGE. I'M ONE OF THE PEOPLE WITHOUT TOO MUCH KNOWLEDGE. I'M PERFECT!"

NOTE: WE HAVE CHOSEN TO FORGO THE TEDIOUS RESEARCH NECESSARY TO LOCATE AN ACTUAL PICTURE OF MS. CARLSON & TO INSTEAD REPRESENT HER, FOR NO PARTICULAR REASON, AS A TALKING CAN OF SPAM.

FINALLY, OF COURSE, THERE ARE **TELEVISION ADS**, WHICH ARE PROBABLY THE **MAIN** SOURCE OF POLITICAL INFORMATION FOR MANY AMERICANS... GOD HELP US...

I'M VOTING FOR THE FELLOW WHO'S GOING TO PUT THE **CRIMINALS** IN **JAIL!**

I'M VOTING **AGAINST** THE GUY WHOSE PICTURE FLOPS BACK AND FORTH!

I'M SUPPORTING THE ONE WITH THAT CATCHY **THEME SONG!**

TOM TOMORROW @ 2-7-96

THIS MODERN WORLD

by TOM TOMORROW

THE INSURGENCY CAMPAIGN OF PAT BUCHANAN IS BEGINNING TO **WORRY** REPUBLICAN PARTY LEADERS.

GOSH--DO YOU MEAN THAT, AFTER SPENDING THE LAST TWO YEARS CHAMPIONING THE POLITICS OF **DIVISIVENESS, RESENTMENT** AND **DEMAGOGUERY**--

--THEIR MOST POPULAR PRESIDENTIAL CANDIDATE TURNS OUT TO BE A **DIVISIVE, RESENTFUL DEMAGOGUE?**

THE POOR **DEARS!** HOW COULD THIS HAVE **HAPPENED?**

REPUBLICANS MAY BE REAPING WHAT THEY HAVE SOWN, BUT THIS IS SCANT CONSOLATION FOR THE REST OF US... AFTER ALL, WHAT DOES IT **SAY**--

--THAT SO MANY AMERICANS WOULD VOTE FOR A MAN WHO HAS CALLED AIDS "GOD'S RETRIBUTION" FOR HOMOSEXUALITY... WHOSE CAMPAIGN STAFF HAS INCLUDED KNOWN WHITE SUPREMACISTS... AND WHOSE WEB PAGE UNTIL RECENTLY FEATURED AN ARTICLE ACCUSING **HILLARY CLINTON** OF BEING AN **ISRAELI SPY**...*

OH GOD, BILL-- TELL ME **MORE!**

MILITARY SECRETS JUST GET ME SO **HOT!**

*WE ARE NOT MAKING THIS UP.

OF COURSE, THE REPUBLICAN ESTABLISHMENT WOULD CERTAINLY BE WILLING TO OVERLOOK SUCH **MINOR UNPLEASANTRIES**--IF NOT FOR BUCHANAN'S **TRULY** UNFORGIVABLE OPPOSITION TO **NAFTA** AND **GATT**...

HE SEEMS TO BELIEVE THAT DOWNSIZING WORKERS AND MOVING FACTORIES OVERSEAS WILL SOMEHOW BE **BAD** FOR THE **ECONOMY!**

GOOD LORD, WHAT A RAVING **LUNATIC!** WHO LET **HIM** OUT OF THE ASYLUM?

111

THIS MODERN WORLD by TOM TOMORROW

Panel 1:

IS THIS A GREAT COUNTRY OR WHAT? AS STEVE FORBES HAS RECENTLY PROVEN, ALL YOU NEED TO BECOME A SERIOUS PRESIDENTIAL CONTENDER IS A VAST PERSONAL FORTUNE, A BLANDLY REPETITIVE MESSAGE, AND THE CHARM AND CHARISMA OF A DISNEYLAND *AUDIO-ANIMATRONIC ROBOT*...

HOPE--GROWTH--AND OPPORTUNITY!

A SIMPLE FLAT TAX! FITS ON A POSTCARD...⟨CLICK⟩...ON A POSTCARD...

⟨CLICK⟩... WHIRRR...

Panel 2:

UNDER HIS PROPOSED FLAT TAX, ALL AMERICANS--RICH OR POOR--WOULD BE SUBJECT TO THE SAME TAX RATE... EXCEPT THAT *INVESTMENT* INCOME WOULD BE COMPLETELY *TAX FREE*...

AND THE RICH, UM, DO TEND TO *HAVE* A BIT MORE INVESTMENT INCOME THAN THE POOR...

SO WHAT'S YOUR POINT?

Panel 3:

MEANWHILE, HILLARY CLINTON IS AGAIN PLAYING THE LEAD ROLE IN THAT RITUALIZED MORALITY PLAY KNOWN AS WHITEWATER...AND PUBLIC OPINION SEEMS SHARPLY DIVIDED BETWEEN TWO SIMPLISTIC EXTREMES...

I THINK SHE IS THE *LIVING EMBODIMENT* OF *EVIL*!

NONSENSE! SHE IS MORE PURE THAN THE *HOLY VIRGIN MOTHER*!

Panel 4:

IT IS, OF COURSE, POSSIBLE THAT SHE IS BEING PERSECUTED UNFAIRLY--*AND* THAT SHE HAS SOMETHING TO HIDE...UNFORTUNATELY, SUCH NUANCES ARE EASILY OVERLOOKED THESE DAYS--PARTICULARLY GIVEN THE TONE SET BY THE *HOUSE FRESHMEN*...

SCHOOL-- I MEAN, GOVERNMENT-- SUCKS!

LET'S SET ALL THE TRASH CANS ON FIRE!

THEN WE CAN MAKE UNCLE NEWT BUY US ALL ICE CREAM!

web: http://www.well.com/user/tomorrow ... Email: tomorrow@well.com ... ©TOM TOMORROW

THIS MODERN WORLD
by TOM TOMORROW

IMAGINE CONGRESS PASSING A LAW MAKING IT ILLEGAL TO MENTION SAFE SEX OR ABORTION IN *NEWSPAPERS* OR ON *TV*... IN FACT, CRIMINALIZING *ANYTHING* THAT MIGHT POSSIBLY BE CONSIDERED "INDECENT" BY ANY OVER-ZEALOUS SMALL TOWN PROSECUTOR IN THE *COUNTRY*... AND THEN IMAGINE THE IMPACT SUCH A LAW WOULD HAVE ON ADULT DISCOURSE IN OUR SOCIETY...

--TONIGHT IN THE CROSSFIRE--A LITTLE ENGINE THAT *THINKS* HE CAN--BUT IS HE JUST *KIDDING HIMSELF*?!

SUCH A LAW *HAS* BEEN PASSED FOR THE *INTERNET*... AS PART OF A SWEEPING REFORM OF THE ENTIRE TELECOMMUNICATIONS INDUSTRY AUTHORED BY LAW-MAKERS WHO--AS FAR AS *WE* CAN TELL--HAVE NEVER TURNED ON A *COMPUTER*... WHICH IS KIND OF LIKE LETTING YOUR *PET CAT* FILL OUT YOUR *TAX RETURNS*...

WHAT DO YOU *THINK*, FLUFFY? ARE WE GOING TO GET A *REFUND* THIS YEAR?

IN A POINTED EDITORIAL THAT HAS BEEN WIDELY DIS-TRIBUTED ONLINE, RETIRED TRIAL JUDGE STEVE RUSSELL PUT IT THIS WAY:

If your children walked by a public park and heard some angry sum-bitches referring to Congress as "the sorriest bunch of cocksuckers ever to sell out the First Amendment" ... no law would be violated ... (but) if they read the same words in cyber-space, they could call the FBI ...

--SIMILARLY, WHILE WE CAN LEGALLY QUOTE JUDGE RUSSELL IN *PRINT*, ONCE THIS CARTOON IS POSTED TO OUR *WEB SITE*, WE WILL BE CONSIDERED *DANGEROUS LAW-BREAKERS*...

UNFORTUNATELY, IN THE WEEKS LEADING UP TO THE BILL'S PASSAGE, OUR NATION'S CORPORATE MEDIA OUTLETS DIDN'T SEEM TO CONSIDER A FULL-FRONTAL ASSAULT ON THE FIRST AMENDMENT PARTICULARLY *NEWSWORTHY*... CONCENTRATING INSTEAD ON THE MORE IMPORTANT QUESTION OF, UM, HOW THE BILL WOULD AFFECT THE PROFITS OF *CORPORATE MEDIA OUTLETS*...

AND BOY ARE WE GONNA RAKE IN SOME DOUGH! BACK TO YOU, BERNIE!

I'M SO HAPPY FOR THEM.

OH YES, ME TOO.

ARE BEAVIS AND BUTTHEAD ON YET?

TOM TOMORROW ©96

web: http://www.well.com/user/tomorrow ... email: tomorrow@well.com

THIS MODERN WORLD

by TOM TOMORROW

MANY AMERICANS BELIEVE THAT THE ANSWER TO SOCIETY'S PROBLEMS IS *SIMPLE*-- WE'VE JUST GOT TO *GET TOUGH ON CRIMINALS*!

LOCK THEM UP AND THROW AWAY THE KEY!

I DON'T KNOW WHY WE DIDN'T THINK OF THIS SOONER!

UNFORTUNATELY LIFE TENDS TO BE A LITTLE MORE COMPLICATED THAN THAT (AS THOSE OF YOU OVER THE AGE OF 15 MAY HAVE NOTICED BY NOW)... AND IN REALITY, MANDATORY SENTENCING LAWS HAVE LED TO ASTONISHING INJUSTICES...

FOR INSTANCE, AS *NEWSWEEK* RECENTLY NOTED, RAPISTS ARE ROUTINELY SET FREE AFTER FOUR YEARS -- BUT A NUMBER OF PRISONERS CONVICTED OF NOTHING MORE SERIOUS THAN SELLING *MARIJUANA* ARE DOING *LIFE WITHOUT PAROLE*...

IN CALIFORNIA, THE PRISON GUARD'S UNION WAS ONE OF THE MAJOR CONTRIBUTORS TO THE "THREE STRIKES" INITIATIVE -- WHICH HAS, OF COURSE, LED TO THE BUILDING OF MORE PRISONS (AND THE HIRING OF MORE GUARDS)... NOW THE HEAD OF THE UNION HAS THE CHUTZPAH TO COMPLAIN THAT PRISONS ARE FILLING UP WITH "HARDCORE CRIMINALS WHO HAVE NO HOPE AND NOTHING TO LOSE..."

--NECESSITATING, COINCIDENTALLY ENOUGH, STILL *MORE* GUARDS...

IS IT JUST *ME*, OR IS THE *TAIL* WAGGING THE *DOG* HERE?

ANOTHER POINT TO CONSIDER IS THAT WHEN THE KEY *HAS* BEEN THROWN AWAY, THE PRISONERS STILL NEED TO BE TAKEN CARE OF... AND AT THIS RATE, OUR NATION'S PRISONS ARE GOING TO START TURNING INTO *RETIREMENT HOMES* WITHIN THE NEXT FEW DECADES...

NURSE... WHAT WAS IT I DID AGAIN?

OH, YOU WERE *VERY BAD* ... YOU SOLD SOME *MARIJUANA* TO SOMEONE, FORTY OR FIFTY YEARS AGO! -- NOW TAKE YOUR MEDICINE FOR ME, OK?

THIS MODERN WORLD

by TOM TOMORROW

Panel 1:

THIS WEEK -- A SPECIAL ANNOUNCEMENT FROM *THIS MODERN WORLD*'S DIRECTOR OF CORPORATE RELATIONS, *BOB FRIENDLY*...

AHEM... IN THE INTEREST OF *EFFICIENCY* AND *COMPETITIVENESS*, WE HAVE DETERMINED IT NECESSARY TO *DOWNSIZE* OUR FORMER CORPORATE MASCOT, *SPARKY THE PENGUIN*!

IT'S BEEN GREAT WORKING WITH YOU, SPARKY! BEST OF LUCK!

WHAT ARE YOU -- *URK*!

Panel 2:

HE'LL CERTAINLY BE MISSED, WON'T HE FOLKS? BUT LET'S NOT DWELL ON THE PAST! TODAY I'D LIKE TO INTRODUCE OUR ZANY *NEW* MASCOT -- *WILBUR THE TALKING STOMACH!* COME ON OUT AND SAY HELLO, WILBUR!

BOY HAVE I GOT BUTTERFLIES IN MY STOMACH! HEY, WAIT A MINUTE -- I *AM* A STOMACH!

Panel 3:

WILBUR COMES TO US FROM OUR FRIENDS AT *MANPOWER, INC**! AS A *CONTINGENCY* EMPLOYEE, HE'LL RECEIVE A MODEST HOURLY WAGE WITH NO BENEFITS -- MAKING HIM *MUCH* MORE COST-EFFECTIVE THAN OUR *FORMER* MASCOT! ADDITIONALLY, WILBUR HAS *ALREADY* SIGNED AWAY ALL MERCHANDISING AND SUBSIDIARY RIGHTS!

I GUESS YOU COULD SAY I'M *HUNGRY* FOR THE WORK! HA, HA! TAKE MY IRRITABLE BOWEL SYNDROME -- *PLEASE*!

*THE NATION'S LARGEST EMPLOYER!

Panel 4:

OF COURSE, WE'D LIKE TO REASSURE OUR READERS THAT THIS RESTRUCTURING WILL IN *NO WAY* IMPACT THE NO-HOLDS-BARRED SATIRE AND POLITICAL COMMENTARY YOU'VE COME TO *EXPECT* FROM *THIS MODERN WORLD*! WE'RE NOT GOING TO PULL ANY PUNCHES, ARE WE, WILBUR?

HECK NO! THOSE POLITICIANS AND STUFF -- THEY TURN MY STOMACH! -- HEY, WAIT A MINUTE -- I *AM* A STOMACH!

I'LL GET YOU FOR THIS, BOB.

UH -- COULD SOMEBODY CALL SECURITY?

TOM TOMORROW © 3-13-96

THIS MODERN WORLD

by TOM TOMORROW

PAT BUCHANAN'S SUPPORTERS HAVE DISMISSED CHARGES THAT THEIR CANDIDATE IS A RACIST DEMAGOGUE AS "NAME CALLING"... AS IF THESE WERE SIMPLY **MEANINGLESS INSULTS** BEING HURLED ABOUT ON THE POLITICAL EQUIVALENT OF A **GRADE SCHOOL PLAYGROUND**...

BUCHANAN IS A **BOOGER-EATER!**

AND HIS FOLLOWERS ARE **GOOBERHEADS!**

THEY ALSO PRETEND IT IS JUST A **WACKY COINCIDENCE** THAT THE BUCHANAN CAMPAIGN ATTRACTS SUCH AN ABSURDLY DISPROPORTIONATE SHARE OF **WHITE SUPREMACISTS, MILITIA MEMBERS,** AND OTHER FAR-RIGHT **HATEMONGERS**...

HEY, PAT'S NO **BIGOT!** HE JUST DOESN'T WANT TO BE PUSHED AROUND BY THE **INTERNATIONAL BANKERS**--IF YOU KNOW WHAT WE **MEAN!**

AND WE THINK YOU **DO!**

THOUGH HIS LEAD IN THE CONTEST IS RAPIDLY BECOMING A MEMORY, BUCHANAN HAS VOWED TO FIGHT ON... DECLARING THAT HE WILL LOOK "LIKE SOMETHING OUT OF **DELIVERANCE**..."

GOSH--YOU MEAN HE PLANS TO EXHIBIT THE STUBBORN DETERMINATION OF A **MURDEROUS BACKWOODS HOMOSEXUAL RAPIST?**

GO, PAT, GO!

MEANWHILE, BOB DOLE'S NOMINATION SEEMS INCREASINGLY INEVITABLE... AND YOU CAN JUST **SENSE** THE EXCITEMENT AMONG THE REPUBLICAN PARTY FAITHFUL...

HIS VISION FOR AMERICA IS, UM, TO HAVE A **BETTER** AMERICA!

HE WANTS TO **IMPROVE** LIFE...UH... RATHER THAN MAKE IT **WORSE!**

HE IS SO INSPIRING, I CAN BARELY CONTAIN MYSELF.

TOM TOMORROW©3-20-96

THIS MODERN WORLD

by TOM TOMORROW

AS YOU MAY RECALL, OUR FORMER CARTOON MASCOT SPARKY THE PENGUIN WAS, UM, *RIGHTSIZED* DURING OUR RECENT CORPORATE RESTRUCTURING ...AND THIS WEEK, WE ARE DELIGHTED TO NOTE THAT HIS REPLACEMENT, WILBUR THE TALKING STOMACH, HAS TAKEN THE COUNTRY BY *STORM!*

GOSH EVERYONE-- MY STOMACH IS JUST DOING *FLIP-FLOPS!*

HEY, WAIT A MINUTE-- I *AM* A STOMACH!

HA, HA!

HA, HA!

HA, HA!

IT'S *WILBURMANIA*, EVERYWHERE YOU LOOK! ADULTS ARE SPENDING THEIR COFFEE BREAKS REPEATING HIS WITTICISMS AND BON MOTS-- WHILE KIDS JUST CAN'T SEEM TO PURCHASE *ENOUGH* WILBUR THE TALKING STOMACH *MERCHANDISE...*

--THEN HE REMEMBERED-- HE *IS* A STOMACH!

HA, HA!

HA, HA!

LOOK--HE DRIPS *SIMULATED STOMACH ACID!*

COOL!

THERE ARE T-SHIRTS AND SCREEN SAVERS AND A PROMOTIONAL TIE-IN WITH A MAJOR FAST FOOD CHAIN...AND, EVEN MORE EXCITING, A *MAJOR MOTION PICTURE* HAS ALREADY BEGUN PRODUCTION--STARRING *ARNOLD SCHWARZENEGGER* AS *WILBUR...*

HEY DIRTBAG--I'M A *STOMACH*--AND I'M GOING TO TEACH *YOU*--

--HOW TO DIGEST *LEAD!*

AND TO THOSE OF YOU WHO HAVE WRITTEN TO EXPRESS YOUR CONCERN ABOUT *SPARKY*--WELL, DON'T WORRY! WE UNDERSTAND HE'S DOING *JUST FINE*...SPENDING TIME WITH *FRIENDS* AND GETTING A CHANCE TO *RELAX...*

...KICKED OUT OF MY OWN STRIP...AND REPLACED BY A *TALKING STOMACH...*

UM, HEY, THAT'S ROUGH. LISTEN, LOVE TO TALK, BUT I GOTTA MEET MY *BROKER...*

COME ON, LET'S DITCH THIS LOSER...

I ♥ WILBUR

TOM TOM-RROW ©3-27-96

To be continued ...

ABOUT THE AUTHOR

Tom Tomorrow is the nom-de-cartoon used by Dan Perkins, who swears, all evidence to the contrary, that he is not a used car dealer in Milford, Connecticut. His weekly cartoon, *This Modern World*, appears regularly in approximately 100 newspapers and magazines, and has been featured in *The Nation*, *The New York Times*, the *Village Voice*, *Spin* magazine, and the *Utne Reader*. He was named one of the Institute for Alternative Journalism's Top Ten Media Heroes of 1992, and has received the Society of Professional Journalists' Freedom of Information Award, the Media Alliance Meritorious Achievement Award for Excellence in Journalism, and (while working in a Midwestern copy center in 1983) the Xerox Corporation's Certificate of Achievement for "Par Excellence" Performance. He is tired of being described by journalists as "bitter," but will accept "pissed off."